10?D
5D

D0966398

The Story of
MARXISM and COMMUNISM

The Story of
MARXISM and
COMMUNISM

by Katharine Savage

Illustrated with photographs and maps

New York   •   *Henry Z. Walck, Incorporated*

I dedicate this book
to Christine and Charles

Acknowledgments

I would like to thank the many friends and also the members of my family who have taken an active part in the preparation of this book. Above all I wish to express great gratitude to Dr. Mark Abrams who read the entire manuscript and from his expert knowledge of the subject gave me invaluable guidance. I have been very fortunate in my advisers, but I alone must accept responsibility for the conclusions contained in the text.

Once more I must pay tribute to Gillian Winger on whose unfailing enthusiasm, energy, and efficiency I depend increasingly.

Thanks are due to the following for permission to use copyright photographs in the illustration of this book:

Camera Press Ltd.: pp. 69, 86, 102, 114, 128, 194 (Rory Dell photo), 207; The John Hillelson Agency Ltd.: pp. 185, 189, 191, 197; Keystone Press Agency Ltd.: pp. 8, 177; Novosti Press Agency: pp. 74, 88, 89, 94, 108, 123, 124, 139, 141, 143, 153, 158, 160, 164, 213; The Observer Picture Library: p. 170 (Rev. Ian Thomson photo); Radio Times Hulton Picture Library: pp. 22, 31, 33, 39, 43, 48, 51, 64, 65, 80, 98, 120, 136; USIS: p. 17; The Wellcome Historical Medical Museum and Library, by courtesy of the Wellcome Trustees: p. 38; Wide World Photos: p. 211. The maps are by Richard Natkiel, F.R.G.S.

Katharine Savage

Contents

The Karl Marx memorial in Highgate Cemetery, London

Introduction

In 1848 Karl Marx, a German historian and philosopher who had been exiled from his own country for his revolutionary views, published the *Communist Manifesto*. This document was originally drawn up in German and later translated into many other languages. The first English edition appeared in 1850. It was a carefully considered analysis of the social evils of Marx's day and an outline of his plans to right the wrongs of the oppressed working people of the world.

The *Communist Manifesto* contained five fundamental ideas. Countless volumes have been written in support of these theories and many others seeking to disprove them. But they are the basic principles of Karl Marx and a starting point for every student of Marxism. Briefly stated they are:

1. From the beginning of human society all history is the history of class struggle. This struggle can only be ended by communism; when the victory of the working class, or proletariat, over the middle class, or bourgeoisie, will set society free once and for all. In a classless world no man will be in a position to exploit another and there will be no cause for conflict.

2. Human beings have progressed through the years from one stage of civilization to another. Feudalism gave way to capitalism; but unfortunately capitalism created modern industry which led to the exploitation of the working class.

3. The working class will, and *must,* become the ruling class.

4. The victory of the working class will inevitably lead to a classless society where the state will wither away.

5. There can be no half measures. Communism is the only system of government with a party program based on the complete overthrow of capitalism. Socialism, in its various forms, is a stage on the road to communism. But it can never be an end in itself for, to the true Marxist, socialism is pointless because it is concerned with the gradual reform of existing conditions instead of total revolution.

These are the basic principles of Marxism; they were followed by the basic aims. In the *Manifesto* Marx clearly stated his determination to abolish private property and inherited wealth so that no man would have the power to force another to work for him; to abolish the bourgeois pattern of family life and parental responsibility so that every child would be educated according to socialist ideals; to abolish nationality so that the working man would have no country; to integrate agriculture and industry so that town and country workers would be united with a common purpose; and to nationalize banks, transport, agriculture, industry and every other communal necessity.

Marx did not disguise his threat to the existing order of life. He called on the proletariat—the factory workers of the world—to arise, destroy the power of their employers, and establish a dictatorship of their own. He ended the *Manifesto* with an outright declaration of class warfare. "The communists disdain to conceal their views and aims. They openly declare that their ends can be attained only by forcible overthrow of all existing conditions. Let the ruling classes tremble at the communist revolution. The proletarians have nothing to lose but their chains. They have a world to win. Workers of all lands unite."

The *Communist Manifesto* became world famous and in time Marx was accepted as the most important figure in the history of revolutionary thought and the founder of the political pattern of life known as Marxism.

Marx proclaimed that the existing state of society was rotten from the roots up and that revolution was inevitable. At the same time he was convinced that revolution could only succeed if the workers fully understood their aims and were prepared to fight for them. He acknowledged socialism as an intermediate stage of society, a steppingstone between capitalism and communism. It was an improvement on capitalism because in a socialist state the rights of the individual were secondary to the needs of the whole community, whereas in capitalism every man was out for himself. Marx predicted that once socialism was established in one country it would lead the way to communism and a worldwide classless society where every nation worked as one, and the people served together, not for themselves or for personal employers, but for the common good.

Karl Marx was of Jewish ancestry, but was brought up in the Christian Church. At the age of sixteen he declared himself an atheist. He denied the existence of God and substituted faith in material progress for religious belief. His dreams of breaking down the barriers of class, leveling incomes, and wiping out the bounds of nationality have not yet come true. Instead Marxism has led to a form of communism which is highly nationalistic and where there are appreciable differences in standards of living. Influenced by intensive propaganda and subject to the harsh direction of party leaders, hundreds of millions of people have abandoned their traditional way of life and the long-established creeds of their forefathers in favor of Marxist-inspired, communist-dictated laws and doctrines.

Social reforms are conceived in the minds of idealists like Karl Marx, but they are shaped by day-to-day events. Both the birth of Marxism and the spread of communism are expressions of the age-old struggle for human happiness and human rights which concerns us vitally.

1 · *The Search for an Ideal State*

IN PRIMITIVE TIMES tribes hunted and fought in family units, each one responsible for its own survival. They existed from day to day with few records of the past and no plans for the future.

Civilization is a product of social development, an organized relationship between individuals, families, communities and nations. Civilized people live according to laws and principles instead of only following instinct. As civilization spread through the world the pattern of life became more disciplined and the pressures more complicated. Groups of families settled in belts of fertile country and began to cultivate the land. On the banks of the Euphrates, the Indus and the Nile, centers of civilization emerged. Tribes gathered together and developed an organized social life and a form of government. These communities were usually composed of nobles, commoners and slaves; they had kings and priests, scholars and soldiers, farmers and merchants, craftsmen and servants. From time to time, even in the best-ordered communities, class distinctions and unequal distribution of wealth caused discontent and strife.

Through the ages, there have always been certain men who were filled with an intense desire to create an ideal state where freedom and justice would prevail and everyone would have equal opportunity. These reformers have, in their various ways, protested against existing evils and sought perfection. Some were religious, concerned with spiritual rather than worldly welfare. Others tried through reason and understanding to establish the land of their dreams.

In the fourth century B.C. Plato, perhaps the greatest of all the Greek philosophers, founded a university in Athens and, in the *Republic* and other writings, set forth his conception of an ideal state. Greek civilization had reached a glorious peak, but Plato looked for even higher standards of moral and political excellence. He pictured a people whose main ambition would be to gain knowledge so that they could rule with unfailing wisdom and justice. In Plato's *Republic* all the members of the community contributed to the common good to the best of their ability and the limit of their strength. The government was in the hands of outstanding natural leaders, especially trained for their duties. The *Republic* therefore was intended to be an example of aristocracy at work in the true sense of the word—the rule of the best. The philosophy of Plato has been a source of inspiration to generation after generation of scholars. His pursuit of personal perfection, his conception of an immortal soul, and faith in an afterlife have had a profound influence on the development of Christian thought for more than two thousand years.

In the sixteenth century Sir Thomas More, an English statesman and a devout and learned Catholic, wrote of an imaginary island where the inhabitants lived under perfect conditions. He called his dream country *Utopia,* a name derived from the Greek word for nowhere. The word has been incorporated into the modern English language to describe a state of perfection which is imaginary and does not really exist. Social and economic life in More's *Utopia* followed closely on the lines of Plato's *Republic:* wealth was communal, education available to all, and everything dedicated to the general welfare. Neither writer had any picture in his mind of a classless society, for both accepted the existence of slavery as a natural feature of a well-organized state.

In the following century there was a civil war in England between the forces of the reigning monarch, Charles I, and an army fighting to protect parliamentary power. Some soldiers of the rebel army formed a republican and democratic group in the name of parliament and the people. This group was called the Levellers by their enemies, who said their aim was "to level men's estates." In fact the Levellers put forward a program of parliamentary and economic reform to improve the lot of the peasant, smallholder and artisan. As political pioneers they appealed to reason rather than set tradition, and as Protestants they demanded religious freedom and the abolition of a state church. The Levellers never succeeded in winning national support, but their proposals marked a turning point in political thought, and their campaign set an example to other reformers in the long struggle for the rights of the common man. The Levellers are now recognized as the first political party in modern Europe.

In England after the Reformation there were a number of devout Protestants who found they could not agree with the strict direction of the Anglican Church. They were ardent Christians, determined to worship according to their own convictions, despite active government persecution. Prominent among these dissenters were the Puritans, so called because of their pious behavior and rigid discipline.

In 1620, in order to escape religious repression, a small but dedicated band of Puritans set sail for North America where they founded a colony later known as Massachusetts. These Christian colonists were resolved to combine their ideas of a perfect church with a perfect state. They planned to establish a model community free from sin and they intended by their "holy experiment" to set a shining example of faultless living to the rest of the Christian world. The Puritans, like the Greeks, laid great stress on education for they believed that good leaders must be learned as well as virtuous. However, when immigrants of other nationalities and different denominations arrived in North America, religious zeal was tempered by political and property interests, and the Puritans were unable to preserve their exclusive order of life and system of government.

By the middle of the eighteenth century, thirteen colonies had been established in North America; and the colonists began to protest against the taxes imposed by the government in London, and to resent being subject to British rule.

Friction mounted between the colonists and the British authorities in North America until, in 1775, open war broke out, and Massachusetts with the twelve other colonies made a joint Declaration of Independence, renouncing their allegiance to Britain.

This historic document was far more than a gesture of defiance or a justification of rebellion, for it presented to the

The signing of the Declaration of Independence, 1776

world a clear statement of the colonists' aims. The Declaration was drafted by Thomas Jefferson, a gifted scholar and statesman from Virginia, the oldest colony. Jefferson was the first spokesman of American political ideals and the real founder of American democracy. He disliked the principle of hereditary aristocracy and believed fervently in individual rights.

The Declaration of Independence claims "that all men are created equal, that they are endowed by their Creator with certain unalienable Rights, that among these are Life, Liberty and the pursuit of Happiness." It is one of the greatest designs for personal freedom, within the bounds of law and order, in the history of the world.

France enthusiastically supported the American Revolution, seizing the opportunity to weaken the power of Britain, her traditional rival. French arms and some French soldiers were dispatched to America and many Frenchmen witnessed the War of Independence at first hand.

In 1781 the last British outpost surrendered and the American colonies were victorious. In every colony the leading citizens set out to construct a separate system of government, using their independence to the full. Most of the authors of these constitutions were educated men, and their knowledge of Greek philosophy and Roman law is evident in their thinking.

In 1787 representatives of the colonies met in the city of Philadelphia and, after considerable discussion, agreed on a Federal Constitution for the United States of America. They set up the apparatus of government, framed laws, levied taxes, abolished titles, proclaimed religious liberty, and laid the foundations for free enterprise and equal opportunity.

American thinking during and after the revolution was strongly influenced by Thomas Paine, a humane and idealistic English writer who emigrated to America and spent many years studying colonial development and constitutional government. In 1791 and 1792 Paine published *The Rights of Man,* expounding his ideals of enlightened rule and his belief in the rights and dignity of the individual, and in the principles of tolerance and freedom of speech.

The United States Constitution was carefully studied by heads of state, politicians, scholars and philosophers in Europe— particularly in France where the government had taken part in liberating the American colonies—and many of its provisions were reflected in the attitudes and actions of future reformers.

At the time when the American states declared their independence, France was a major European power. The court at Versailles had set a fashion in magnificence and manners for over a century, and French was the common diplomatic language of the continent. The country had plentiful agricultural resources, the main source of wealth in that day. But the distribution of the land was mainly feudal, with large estates owned by the king, the nobles and high-ranking clergy; and cultivated by the peasants, often by a system of forced labor. In general the landowners were rich, and they were largely exempt from taxation; while the peasants were very poor indeed, frequently on the verge of starvation, yet subject to heavy taxes.

In the eighteenth century revolutionary ideas were spreading, and an undercurrent of savage discontent ran beneath the glittering surface of French life. Already, expanding commerce and increasing culture had created a new class of society in Europe. Attracted by the prospect of a better way of life, ambitious peasants had left the land and gone into business. They were able and energetic; they congregated in the towns and cities and took charge of trade and industry. They formed a prosperous middle class, or bourgeoisie, between the aristocracy and the peasantry. Successful bourgeois became lawyers and doctors, bankers and merchants, writers and craftsmen, and included in their numbers many of the most able men in France. They were not, in general, revolutionaries, for they were mostly well-to-do and had become comparatively secure. But gradually they developed a school of philosophical and humanitarian writing which revealed deep resentment of the unfair privilege enjoyed by the monarchy, the nobility and the Church. They put into words the longing of hard-working honest citizens for equal political rights, just taxation and a chance to make good.

Prominent among these reformers was Voltaire, a brilliant poet, playwright, wit, satirist and philosopher. He smarted under the injustice and tyranny that dominated French life and demanded liberty of speech, action and worship.

Another passionate and eloquent advocate of human freedom was the French-Swiss writer Jean Jacques Rousseau, who put forward the theory that man is born neither good nor bad, but that his character is molded by social environment. He believed that inequalities of wealth and complex pressures of a modern state produced individual frustration and moral confusion. In 1762 Rousseau published *Du Contrat Social (Of Social Contract)*, describing a personal ideal that men could attain harmony and liberty by making a social contract among themselves. He claimed that no community could be united unless the citizens shared certain fundamental beliefs and everyone had an opportunity to take an equal part in government. He believed that laws must be made for the equal benefit of all, that goodness must be recognized and rewarded, and that people could be on good terms with their neighbors only if they enjoyed personal liberty and were first at peace with themselves.

Voltaire and Rousseau differed in their attitude to religion. Voltaire openly mocked the Church while Rousseau regarded it as a valuable moral force. But both reformers criticized the clergy, who had grown lazy and luxury-loving, and deplored the fact that even the bishops, who had their own palaces and lived like princes, were exempt from taxation. Neither Voltaire nor Rousseau approved of violence or preached revolution, but they opened peoples' eyes to the wrongs of society, and undermined respect for the ruling classes.

When Louis XVI came to the French throne in 1774 he inherited a country seething with unrest, and a treasury bankrupt through corruption and mismanagement. Almost everyone was critical of the monarchy: the aristocrats and the bourgeoisie because they had no hand in the government; and the poorer townspeople and peasants because, in the face of the gross extravagance of the upper classes, they were penniless and hungry. The young king was well meaning, but he entirely lacked the capacity to enforce the measures which might have saved the monarchy. His fumbling attempts to improve the Constitution ended in complete failure, and as reforms did not come from above, revolution burst out from beneath.

On July 14, 1789, a ragged mob armed with stolen weapons stormed the Bastille—an ancient fort converted into a political prison—on the outskirts of Paris. This was a signal for widespread revolt. The king was unable to restore order and he surrendered his authority to a National Assembly composed of representatives of all classes of society who had been hurriedly summoned to give France a new constitution. In 1791 this body published this Constitution, prefaced by a glowing Declaration of the Rights of Man which had much in common with the American Declaration of Independence and contained the es-

The storming of the Bastille, 1789

sence of many long-overdue reforms. At this time Thomas Paine was in Paris, in close touch with the revolutionary leaders. In his own work on *The Rights of Man* he defended the purpose of the French Revolution and advocated republican rule.

But the voices of reason and moderation were soon drowned by a mounting wave of violence, when the Jacobins— the most extreme revolutionaries—gained power by a skillful campaign of rabble-rousing. In 1792 France was declared a republic, and in 1793 the king was executed by revolutionary command. To the stirring music of the "Marseillaise," the newly composed national anthem of the revolution, soldiers and civilians marched together, with red, white and blue cockades on their caps and guns in their hands.

During the following twelve months a reign of terror gripped the country. In Paris alone more than two thousand men and women died at the guillotine as a penalty for their noble birth and possession of property. Many of them displayed remarkable gallantry, but once the masses took charge they had no mercy for their oppressors. This was unrestricted class warfare and every aristocrat was an enemy. In the name of Liberty, Equality and Fraternity, the peasants and the working class—or proletariat—took its revenge for centuries of oppression and neglect. In 1794, when the terror died down, France entered into five years of indecisive government until Napoleon Bonaparte became First Consul and later Emperor of the French people. After Napoleon's downfall in 1815 royal restorations and counter-revolutions modified the Constitution. In 1958 General Charles de Gaulle, leader of the French Resistance during World War II, proclaimed a Fifth Republic.

Some British statesmen at first viewed the French Revolution with a measure of approval; and when the news of the fall of the Bastille reached America the revolutionaries were hailed as liberators. Many freedom-loving people were in favor of a movement to weaken the absolute supremacy of the French monarchy. However, as the new republic lapsed into unbridled savagery, the approval turned to horror and fear that the spirit of violent revolution might spread.

The French Revolution made its greatest impact on Russia. From 1762–1796 this vast empire was ruled by Catherine II, a highly intelligent and cultured woman. Early in her reign she had been in touch with Voltaire and other men of outstanding talent and vision and had seen the need for drastic changes in social relations within Russia. But when Catherine tried to improve the state of the serfs in her own country she met stubborn opposition from the owners of the big estates. After the butchery of the French Revolution the disillusioned empress turned her back on reform and punished severely anyone who expressed advanced opinions of any kind. At the end of the eighteenth century, while serfdom had almost disappeared in western Europe, the Russian peasants were worse off than ever before. They rebelled in desperation, but every uprising was crushed by imperial armies.

Rebellion in America had been sparked by resentment at British domination, and in France by despair at social injustice. Neither revolution was socialist-inspired. There was no talk of a communal regime, and the basic socialist doctrines of public ownership and state control were hardly considered in revolutionary circles on either side of the Atlantic. They had no public appeal: the American dream of an ideal state was one where every colonist was free to make good in his own way, and the French reformers pictured a country where the citizens had unrestricted opportunity and every peasant owned a farm.

However, the French Revolution was a landmark in the history of socialism for it destroyed a monarchy, planted the seeds of revolutionary thought in other countries, and proved both a stimulus and a warning to future revolutionary leaders. But its greatest contribution to the socialist cause was the demonstration of the uncontrollable power of a proletariat, backed up by a peasantry, fully aroused to anger.

In the *Communist Manifesto* Karl Marx recognized the French Revolution as a historical change, abolishing feudal property in favor of bourgeois property. He did not consider it a major victory, but merely a stage of social development, which was likely to whip up class hatred and lead to world revolution.

2 · *The World of Karl Marx*

AT THE TIME of the French Revolution the territories which later formed the German Empire were divided into a number of separate kingdoms, principalities and dukedoms. Each state was ruled by an independent sovereign, all-powerful in his own realm. These hereditary dictators made the laws of the land, decided how their subjects should worship, and called them to arms at will. As a result there was massive discontent among the lower classes of society who were forced to obey these highhanded commands. They grudged paying taxes which brought them no reward, and they were tired of fighting wars for causes that did not concern them. By the beginning of the nineteenth century many enlightened and foresighted Germans were working for national unity. They were members of a political group known as "liberals." They believed in gradual reform and the right of ordinary people to take part in government. They hoped that a central parliament with freely elected representatives from all the different states would curb the power of the autocratic rulers, compel them to grant constitutional reforms and to acknowledge the right of ordinary men and women to personal liberty and some share in the government.

Prominent among the freethinkers and philosophers of this time was Georg Hegel. He was born at Stuttgart in Prussia in 1770, and grew up in an atmosphere of political unrest. His student years were colored by news of revolution and talk of reform. Hegel's parents wanted him to enter the Church; but, although he read theology at college, he decided not to become a minister. Instead, he found part-time work as a tutor so that he could have leisure to study philosophy, Greek literature, history and politics. Although Hegel did not agree with the orthodox religious teaching of his day, he never doubted the existence of an infinite God, and the unity of the divine and human. In his writings he used the German word *Geist* which means mind as well as spirit. He set himself the task of comprehending the workings of the universe, and in time developed a social philosophy based on Christian doctrines combined with the reasoning of the great Greek sages.

Hegel adopted from the Greeks the idea of the dialectic as a means of arriving at pure truth. The term dialectic is derived from the Greek word *dialego,* meaning to discuss or debate. Later Karl Marx, the originator of the doctrine of Marxism, investigated and accepted the theory of the dialectic and made it a dominant factor in his social philosophy. Marx agreed with Hegel and the Greeks that a discussion which permits different points of view to oppose and contradict each other is the best means of clearing away misconceptions and discovering the absolute truth. Moreover Marx saw the world as a perpetual collision of conflicting forces merging eventually into a union of opposites. He respected contradictions as a spur to progress, for he believed that without the clash of positive and negative, reality and idealism, good and evil, life would go on in exactly the same way from year to year and century to century. Everything would be repeated and there would be no reason for change or pressure for advancement.

Hegel maintained that human history was gradually carrying out God's purpose, that civilized states were expressions of God's will, and that through the ages mankind had made great spiritual and moral progress. He was convinced that the time had come for people to achieve their highest aims, escape from the slavery of violence and ignorance, and attain human freedom.

While Marx adopted Hegel's theory of the dialectic, he consistently denied the existence of any divine power, and he did not share Hegel's faith in the state as an instrument of social improvement. Instead, he was convinced that class struggle was the irresistible force destined by history to create violent upheavals, and that these upheavals would lead to universal harmony.

Hegel's frail appearance contrasted sharply with the vigor of his mind. He had a vision of absolute truth and he defended it with confidence. When he held the chair of philosophy at Berlin University his students were fascinated by the depth of his discussions. His quest for reform followed the spirit of the times, and he gathered a devoted following. His writings were widely read in his native Prussia, in France and Italy, and later in Britain. Hegel died in 1831 and for a time interest in his theories declined. But when it became apparent how greatly the Hegelian system of philosophy had influenced the political thinking of Karl Marx, it gained fresh momentum.

In 1830, the year before Hegel's death, there were widespread revolutionary outbreaks in Europe. Parisians rose against the reactionary policies of the monarchy which had been restored after the fall of Napoleon Bonaparte; in Brussels the Catholic Belgians rebelled against Protestant Dutch sovereignity; in Warsaw Polish patriots fought desperately to free themselves from Russian imperial rule; and in Italy soldiers led an armed revolt against Austrian occupation and the dominance of the Roman Catholic Church. Everywhere, except in France, the uprisings were sternly suppressed for the time being, and the existing regimes continued. But once the fires of liberal thought were kindled, it was hard to put them out. They smoldered underground until, in 1848, they flared up once more in France, Hungary, Italy and Germany. Marx and his followers had already been working on a program to overthrow capitalist governments and they hoped that this was the beginning of the end of capitalism.

Karl Marx was born in 1818 in the ancient town of Trier which lies in Prussia, not far from the French frontier. Both his parents were Jewish, and his father was a lawyer who spent a great deal of time studying philosophy and religion. Before Karl's birth, the whole family renounced Judaism, embraced Christianity, and were baptized as Protestants.

As Trier lay so close to France many refugees, homeless from the French Revolution, had crossed the frontier and settled there. Consequently, from his boyhood Karl Marx was exposed to heated controversy on the causes and results of revolution. After leaving school he attended the universities of Bonn and Berlin where he discovered the works of Hegel. He developed socialist ideas early in life and soon renounced Christianity. For a time he wanted to be a poet, but he turned from poetry to philosophy because it seemed to offer a firmer foundation for socialist theories. He chose journalism as a career and in 1842, at the age of twenty-four, he became editor of a Cologne newspaper with a liberal policy.

The following year Marx married Jenny von Westphalen, whom he had known since his school days and who was the daughter of a high-ranking government official. They loved each other deeply and her devotion did not falter in long years of poverty and exile. Soon after his marriage Marx's newspaper was suppressed because of his outspoken criticism of social conditions in Prussia and of the Protestant Church. He and his wife left Germany and moved to Paris. He chose the French capital mainly because he knew that at this time the city was a center of intense socialist activity. The Comte de Saint-Simon, founder of French socialism, had been dead for nearly twenty years, but his followers had developed a school of thought to study his theories. They recognized two opposing factors in the history of philosophy: the first, destructive, characterized by war and selfishness; the second, constructive, characterized by obedience and partnership and controlled by religious belief. The Simonites approved of abolishing the laws of inheritance and transferring all property to the state. But they also believed in a seniority of merit and virtue; that men and women should be rewarded according to their capacity and the quality of their work.

Marx believed in social and economic equality in all things

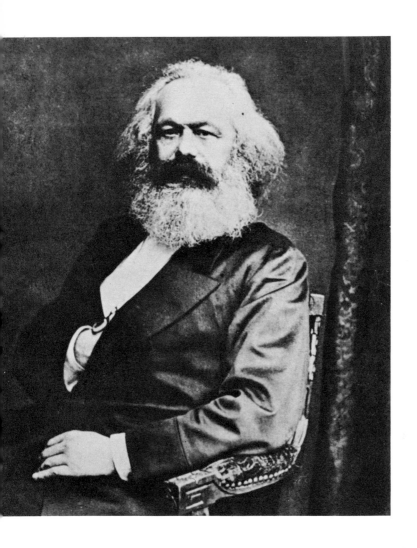

Karl Marx

and he bitterly disagreed with the school of Saint-Simon on the question of award for individual merit. He also refused to consider seriously the doctrines of François Fourier, a contemporary of Saint-Simon, who blamed the innumerable restraints of everyday life for the vice and unhappiness in the world. Fourier claimed that if human beings were able to gratify their natural passions and desires they would find personal fulfillment and therefore create social harmony. He also evolved a scheme to divide society into departments, or phalanges, each containing about sixteen hundred people who would share the industrial, agricultural and domestic work, and receive a part of the profits. In the nineteenth century a number of phalanges were founded, over forty in the United States alone, to carry out Fourier's social experiment. They failed, however, through lack of leadership and efficient organization.

Marx considered Saint-Simon and Fourier impractical and over-idealistic, and it was probably during this period in Paris that he developed the contempt for utopian schemes and gradual social reform which he expressed so fiercely in his later writings. Marx also attacked the teaching of the contemporary French social reformer Pierre Proudhon, and an antagonism arose between the two men which mounted through the years.

While Marx was in Paris he met Friedrich Engels, a German social philosopher of about his own age, who held many of the same ideas. The two men formed a close friendship and working partnership which lasted until Marx died. In 1848 they had both moved to Brussels and were working out the fundamental principles of Marx's social philosophy in preparation for the *Communist Manifesto*.

Friedrich Engels

By this time the campaign for German unity had gained active support, and in May 1848 a number of German liberals conferred and summoned representatives from the various states to the Prussian city of Frankfurt for consultation. In Germany in 1848, and later in many other European countries, the liberals formed a middle party between autocratic rulers who were striving to keep power and wealth in the hands of a privileged few, and socialists who stood for revolution and common ownership. At St. Paul's Church in Frankfurt the liberals appointed a preliminary parliament and made plans to elect a national assembly to govern a united Germany. They hoped by this means to end the wars which had torn apart the German-speaking people, and to build a new nation through peaceful discussion. The Frankfurt Parliament was composed of learned, honorable and patriotic men sharing a common purpose and prepared to surrender local privileges for the common good. But they did not have the backing of the heads of state who clung stubbornly to their regal positions and would not consider any loss of personal power. The architects of German unity were also confronted by the complex problems of deciding where the boundaries of their new empire would lie, and of collecting money to pay for their projected reforms.

While the deliberations continued at Frankfurt, Frederick William IV, King of Prussia, faced outright rebellion in Berlin. For seven years, in response to popular demand, he had toyed with ideas of reforming the Constitution and giving the people a freely elected parliament, but he had achieved nothing. Finally the Berliners reached the end of their patience, barricaded the streets and fired on the servants of the crown. King Frederick

William quelled the uprising with renewed promises of reform and a proclamation of German unity. In April 1849 the National Assembly at Frankfurt offered him the crown of a German Empire. Prussia was the strongest of the north German states and it seemed appropriate that she should take the lead. Frederick William refused the offer because it was not supported by the German princes. He was an autocrat at heart and he was not prepared to side with the champions of reform against the existing order.

When they failed to find a leader, the liberals could not carry out their plans, the National Assembly petered out and the hope of peace and prosperity died away. The golden opportunity to unite Germany by compromise and good will was lost forever. Union was only achieved by years of bloodshed and suffering.

With the upsurge of reformist ideas, Karl Marx had been allowed to return to Germany. But after the final collapse of the Frankfurt Parliament he and other outright socialists were expelled by reactionary rulers who clung to their pre-Frankfurt policies. Marx went to England where he spent the remainder of his life in dire poverty. At the same time many more moderate reformers, feeling that they could accomplish little in Germany, emigrated to America where they could live with their families according to democratic principles, and take an active part in promoting the development and steering the course of a great new nation.

3 · *The Workshop of the World*

AFTER YEARS OF STUDY, Karl Marx came to the conclusion that there was no better way of improving society than by outright revolution. Marxism, therefore, became a mixture of theory and practice because Marx's work transformed socialism from an idealistic doctrine into an active political movement.

When Marx published the *Communist Manifesto,* an industrial revolution had changed the traditional way of life in many European countries, and most of all in England where Marx made his home for the last thirty-four years of his life. With increasing speed and efficiency, factories were mass-producing for international markets goods which had formerly been laboriously handmade for local use. In industry and commerce the British people were fifty years ahead of the most advanced continental nations and the country was renowned as "the workshop of the world." When Queen Victoria came to the throne in 1837 England was extremely powerful, prosperous and at peace with other nations.

Cotton and coal had been two main sources of British

wealth. The raw cotton was imported first from American plantations and later from India and Egypt. The moist English climate was well suited to the cotton industry. The early cotton mills were built on riverbanks where the wheels were turned by water power. Then in 1769 a Scottish inventor named James Watt devised a condenser which in time made steam power the driving force in industry. It was no longer necessary to build cotton mills beside running water and it became more practical and economical to concentrate production in populated areas. In the north and midlands of England new industrial towns sprang up and textile factories multiplied.

Large deposits of coal in England and Wales had been known of for some time, but it was only toward the end of the eighteenth century that people realized the coal could be used as fuel to transform industry. Mining companies were formed, engineers sank deep shafts, and thousands of miners worked underground in appalling conditions. Small children were sent down into the mines and harnessed to coal trolleys because they could haul them through tunnels too low for men to pass. Soon a network of canals and railways was constructed to carry the coal from the pitheads to the towns. Coal replaced charcoal in forges and blast furnaces, and, as cotton manufacturers had moved away from the rivers, now iron and steel manufacturers left the woods where they had previously cut down trees to make charcoal. They congregated near the coal mines and very soon whole areas were grimed with smoke and coal dust. In this "black country," British companies manufactured machinery and began to sell it to buyers all over the world.

Children working in the coal mines

The social effects of this industrial progress were enormous. Cottage workshops and village industries began to disappear and people left the land to take jobs in the towns and cities. They

The Black Country

arrived poor and friendless and their only asset was their capacity to work. Often they were mercilessly exploited by factory owners who made fortunes for themselves by paying their employees a bare living wage and selling goods at a huge profit. Marx condemned this power of capital over labor as an unqualified evil.

But, apart from the prospect of a factory job, there was another compelling reason for people to leave the countryside. The smallholders and farm hands were driven out by the enclosure of open land. Formerly, farmers with an acre or two had used them to grow crops and had exercised their right to graze their herds of cows and flocks of sheep on commons which they shared with the rest of the village. Now well-to-do lords of the manor and successful farmers were taking possession of the grazing grounds and fencing them in for their own use. The commons disappeared and the English landscape took on the checkerboard appearance that it still has today.

Farming became more efficient because landlords had enough property to employ a method of crop rotation which preserved the richness of the land. The food supply increased, but at the same time the small farmers found that they could not earn a living. To make matters worse the mechanical inventions of the flying shuttle and the spinning jenny took the wool business out of the hands of cottage spinners and weavers and transferred it to town factories, so whole families were out of work.

In country communities many people had been poor and hungry, but local squires had often kept a fatherly eye on their tenants and helped them when times were bad. It had been healthy working outdoors and village amusements were cheap and simple. In the new factory towns the living conditions were appalling. Employers put up houses for their factory hands, but seldom had any personal contact with them. These tenement buildings and rows of jerry-built houses were shamefully overcrowded. Large families lived in one room in the utmost squalor without proper lighting or heating, running water or drainage. Slum areas surrounded every factory; the streets were filthy and the street lights so dim and far apart that it was not safe to go out at night for fear of cutthroats and robbers. There was no effective police force and criminals were hardly ever caught and punished. Existing schools and social services were totally inadequate. The Church of England was very short of clergymen and few of them were willing or able to cope with this mass misery. Only the nonconformist sects, such as the Methodists, Wesleyans and Quakers, sent their ministers to comfort and care for the poor.

Factory conditions were similarly bad. Men, women and children were used as "sweated labor," overworked and underpaid. They toiled day and night because there were no laws to limit working hours. Trade unions were illegal until 1824 so the workers had no means of expressing their grievances. Little children were taken from orphanages and some were even hired out by their own destitute parents. They were put to work with the rest. It was not until 1847 that the Ten Hours Act passed through Parliament, restricting the working hours of young children and boys and girls up to the age of eighteen.

While new machines revolutionized industry, new scientific discoveries challenged orthodox religious teaching. In 1859 Charles Darwin published his *Origin of Species* and presented the theory of organic evolution, or the gradual development of human from lower forms of animal life. He described the process of natural selection and the consequent survival of the fittest physical types. The upholders of established religion believed that all creation was a miracle accomplished through divine power, and they bitterly opposed Darwin's theories. Karl Marx and a number of his contemporary reformers were atheists. They had discarded the religious teaching of their childhood and denied the existence of a God, so they readily accepted the scientific explanation of the origin of man. Therefore, in nineteenth-century Europe, both spiritual and social values were in a state of conflict and revision.

For families of means this nineteenth century was a splendid era. The aristocracy and gentry owned country estates and also made fortunes from comparatively poor land developed for factories and coal mines. A new middle class, the British bourgeoisie, was created by the demands of expanding trade. Each year there were more manufacturers, merchants, engineers, lawyers, bankers, accountants, shippers and shopkeepers. Their standard of living soared and their horizons widened. The apparent prosperity was so great, the advances in mechanical invention so dramatic, the discoveries of science so impressive, and the commercial position of Britain so predominant that most people were dazzled. They accepted wealth as a matter of course and poverty as the inevitable price of progress. Even the most responsible and well-intentioned leaders of public life tended to ignore the plight of the factory workers without whom this industrial success could never have been achieved.

However, there were men well aware of the injustice and inequality prevailing in a large section of English life. Early in the century Robert Owen, a Welshman of humble birth and

Robert Owen's settlement at New Lanark

little formal education, set an example in factory reform. He managed a large cotton factory in the Scottish town of New Lanark and ran it according to his own high principles. Owen introduced education and sanitation; he encouraged cleanliness, orderliness and thrift, paid his workers an honest wage and took an interest in their welfare. The experiment finally broke down because Owen's partners were not satisfied with the 6 per cent profit which he considered right and just.

Later in life Robert Owen developed a wholly socialistic scheme to found settlements where parents handed their children over to community upbringing after the age of three, and everything was run on a common basis. He visualized a world with these communities spreading until all mankind shared the same interests. Although his plans were impractical, Owen's thinking —like that of many other reformers of his time—had an effect on the shaping of socialism.

In the 1840's Richard Cobden, an able cotton salesman and practical businessman, made a determined attack on social suffering. In his travels through the industrial towns of England he witnessed the desperate hunger and unhappiness of the working people. He launched a crusade to repeal the Corn Laws which had raised the price of bread. Cobden fought for free trade, against bitter opposition, until the government was forced to recognize his demands and housewives were able to buy cheaper bread.

The members of the first organized working-class movement in Britain were known as Chartists because they compiled the People's Charter, published in 1838. The Charter was based on six points, all designed to give the ordinary working man the vote, which only the upper and middle classes then possessed. The Chartists hoped that this reform would lead to a rightful representation in Parliament, and that social and economic evils would consequently be remedied. They drafted their proposals in a year of industrial depression with heavy unemployment and widespread hardship, and they won considerable support in many factory towns. But Parliament refused to discuss Chartist aims and soon dissension arose in Chartist ranks. Some leaders favored working-class advancement through moderate and parliamentary means, others put their faith in riots and strikes to gain their ends. In the mid-nineteenth century conditions began to improve and Chartism petered out.

But there was still a tremendous gulf between low wages and high profits, and to rebels like Karl Marx and Friedrich Engels it seemed that the whole unbalanced system of society should be condemned to destruction.

Karl Marx and his disciples publicized the urgent need for drastic change, and preached a form of socialism which could only be brought about through class warfare. This political creed, known as Marxism after its founder, was designed to liberate the factory workers of the most advanced nations from capitalist oppression. In fact, contrary to Marx's expectations, the *Communist Manifesto* failed to arouse the industrial proletariat of western Europe.

In England—the most advanced industrial nation in the world at that time—reform came slowly; not through the class war that Marx predicted, but through an awakened social conscience and the liberal outlook of parliamentary leaders. As the nineteenth century wore on, successive British governments passed laws to give more people the vote, protect labor, promote education, clear the slums, and provide for the sick, the aged and the destitute.

4 · *The Meaning of Marxism*

WHEN KARL MARX ARRIVED in London in 1849 with his wife and young family he was thirty-one years old, out of work, exiled from his own country and desperately poor. He managed to earn a few pounds a year by writing for the New York *Tribune,* but he was otherwise entirely dependent on the generosity of Friedrich Engels, his fellow philosopher and friend.

Marx took two rooms in Soho, a district largely populated by foreigners, where the lodgings were simple and the rents low. Nevertheless he was constantly in debt, his wife lived in daily fear of the bailiffs, and they repeatedly pawned their household possessions and even their clothes. to pay for food. Lenchen, the faithful servant who stayed with them for forty years, very often worked without wages.

They were a devoted family and Marx was brokenhearted when, during these years of hardship, two of his children, a son and daughter, died. Later he faced another tragedy, for his only remaining son died also.

Engels, the son of a German textile manufacturer, came to England in 1849 to manage the Manchester branch of the thriving family firm. It was ironic that, in order to provide his family with the bare necessities of life and continue the work on which he had set his heart, Marx accepted money made from the textile business, a part of the industrial system that he detested and was determined to destroy. Engels and Marx could hardly have been more different in character, outlook and position. Although Marx criticized other philosophers for their impractical ideas, he was himself a dreamer and an idealist, a somber melancholy genius possessed by an insatiable desire to revolutionize mankind. He was a profound thinker, ever probing into the background of social problems, seeking evidence to support his convictions, but never wholly satisfied with his findings. Year after year he spent long days in the reading room of the British Museum, studying the development of philosophy, history and economics in ancient and modern civilizations and trying to apply his knowledge to nineteenth-century Britain. His evenings he devoted to conspiracy and debate, and his home became a meeting place for political exiles and budding revolutionaries. He never really mastered the English language, but he was an intense and impassioned speaker, abruptly overruling any views that did not fit his own. Consequently he made many enemies and few friends. Gradually his health broke down under the strain of his research and poverty, but he still worked on.

Engels on the other hand was cheerful and friendly, less intellectual but far more practical. Through his factory experience he gained firsthand knowledge of industrial conditions which he handed on to Marx. He received a steady income, and made no secret of the fact that he enjoyed the luxuries of life. But, despite their contrasting temperaments, the two philosophers shared a

A London slum in the mid-nineteenth century

strong sense of purpose and each contributed something the other lacked to a partnership which lasted for forty years.

Marx devoted his life to making a systematic analysis of universal society, and to an attempt to give the proletariat an understanding of its rightful place in the world. Together he and Engels turned social philosophy into a powerful weapon of class warfare. They set out to arm the factory workers with revolutionary ideas, based on what they claimed was a scientific study of the natural laws of human society. They applied past experience to present issues and urged the masses to fulfill a historical mission by breaking down class barriers so that every man could become master of his own future.

Marx had already discarded the spiritual beliefs which had formed the foundation of religious teaching and set the standards of European morals and behavior for many centuries. He taught that men should no longer put their trust in God. Instead they should take the responsibility for their own actions, have faith in themselves, and strive for personal freedom within a socialist state.

A basic section of Marxist doctrine is now known as "dialectical materialism." This complicated title can be translated into simpler terms. While Marx and Engels accepted Hegel's theories on the value of contradictory debate and the force of opposites, they also proclaimed their own belief in the might of material things and the supremacy of matter over mind.

They accepted the continuous struggle between old and new, past and future, positive and negative, as part of the inevitable forward and upward movement of human development. They saw the universe as a compromise of contradictions. They defined the never-ending process of universal change as a sequence of "thesis, antithesis, synthesis," meaning that something that is laid down is challenged by something directly opposite and the outcome is the result of a combination of the two.

Marx felt most strongly that the laws of thinking and living must correspond to existing material conditions, that it is useless to plan for perfection and neglect reality. Policy must be flexible and readily adapted to current circumstances. For instance, he thought that the British factory workers were right to accept a ten-hour day in 1847, because it was the best concession they could expect to get at that time. But they were also right not to be satisfied with it indefinitely, because when they gained more power, they would need greater leisure to use it wisely. Therefore the proof of a sound society was its ability to move with the times.

Dialectical materialism pictures the world not as matter divided into myriads of independent atoms, but as matter involved in mass movement and part of a continual succession of processes and changes. The Marxist argument follows that, as matter is always in motion, it arrives, exists for a period, and then dies away. Also, it is only important in its relationship to other matter, just as single human beings are unimportant alone and only worthy of serious consideration in their relationships to one another.

Dialectical materialism supports the scientific discoveries of Darwin, tracing living organisms through a long span of evolution until they finally emerged as man. Marx goes on from Darwin to the assumption that together man and matter form society. Marx knew from his reading that as the social structures of the human race took shape, man passed from the stages of primitive communism, to feudalism and thence to capitalism. He considered each stage an essential preparation for the next, and each in turn was compelled to give way to its successor and fade out of existence. He looked ahead to a future stage when, in the inevitable procession of history, capitalism would be forced to

Industrial progress in Britain

surrender to socialism, and, in the course of time, to the Marxist ideal—a universal stateless, classless society. In Marx's day the terms socialism and communism had an identical meaning. It was not until the Russian Revolution that there was a clear-cut separation between the term communism, which meant a Marxist revolutionary state of society, and socialism, which was applied to various aspects of social reform. Later Lenin spoke of socialism as a stage on the road to pure communism and the classless society.

Marx regarded production as the basis of human society; for man must find food, clothing and shelter before he can think, develop, progress, or even breathe. Without production society would perish, and production can only be achieved by an alliance of man and matter. Man is the force, and matter is the source of production. Marx contended that the essentials of life are not free gifts of nature. They have first to be earned and then successfully distributed. This process of manufacture and exchange is known as industry. As populations grew and scientific knowledge improved, industry played an increasingly important part in social life. Marx viewed the Industrial Revolution as the inevitable outcome of the age-old struggle of man against the forces of nature, and welcomed the advance from primitive stone tools to modern machinery as clear evidence that man was slowly gaining the upper hand.

Marx's main aim was to change the then existing pattern of production, not through the course of gradual reform, but by swift, decisive revolution. He constantly stressed the injustice of a capitalist system where the means of production is held by the aristocracy and the bourgeoisie, small privileged minorities, while the force of production is provided by the proletariat, a large underpaid majority. And he condemned a society which allowed the exploitation of man by man and the unequal distribution of wealth.

The real value of labor is a complex subject. Many political economists before Marx have studied it, and many since. Marx supported the theory that the selling price of any commodity, whether it is a steam engine, a ton of wheat, or a pocket handkerchief, should be equal to the value of the labor that has gone into its making. In fact he insisted that the value of the labor *is* the value of the finished product. Human effort creates wealth, and wealth can only be measured by human effort. The two are inseparable.

Marx carried the reasoning further, for he criticized the

capitalists because they sold the steam engines, wheat and hand-kerchiefs for far more than the cost of the wages they paid their workers, and pocketed the difference. He denounced the factory owners as "profiteers" because they grew rich on other men's work.

Common ownership is the essence of true socialism. Under ideal socialist conditions production is no longer undertaken for personal profit; no worker is forced to work for a private employer and sell his manpower in exchange for a bare living; and no employer of labor has the right or the opportunity to make money out of another man's skill and endurance. Only the state has the right to employ labor and collect profits. Industry yields fair shares for all on the principle of "from each according to his abilities, to each according to his needs." Marx predicted that in such a state the class hostility aroused by unequal standards of living would disappear, and the means of production would be developed for the general welfare. He estimated that with modern machinery and efficient techniques, there would be plenty for all, and no need for poverty.

Marx and Engels stressed the challenge of the *Communist Manifesto:* "In place of the old bourgeois society, with its classes and class antagonisms, we shall have an association in which the free development of each is the condition for the free development of all."

Marx spoke frequently of the right of every man to gain personal freedom; for he believed that a sense of freedom is a vital quality in the makeup of all human beings. He regarded this freedom not as a Heaven-sent gift of God, but as something that has to be won gradually through social activity. "Men make their lives. But they do not make them just as they wish."

While Thomas Jefferson in the Declaration of Independence pictured the establishment of freedom as a result of enlightened man-made laws, Marx and Engels saw freedom as a result of social understanding and a working partnership with the laws of nature. They presented communism as the realization of freedom and the successful conclusion of the conflict between man and nature.

Marx, like Plato and many other students of the universe, sought the real meaning of truth. To Marx, truth appeared to be a meeting of ideas and reality. He believed that it was seldom exact and lasting, and that few statements are absolutely true. Most are only approximate and need to be revised and restated in the light of new learning. Marx recognized that scientific progress can disprove what had previously seemed to be indisputable fact, and every stage of knowledge, like every stage of society, is a steppingstone to the next. Because some apparent truths turn out to be falsehoods, and some lies contain a large measure of truth, they should all be taken into account. Marxism claimed to be critical and practical, geared to the irresistible changes in human affairs, and always looking ahead.

But although Marx dedicated his whole being to forging a spearhead of revolution, he himself never played a prominent part in British labor politics. He did, however, take a hand in starting a workingman's association known as the First International. This organization was formed for the purpose of bringing together labor leaders from all the European countries. In

1864, in London, Marx delivered the Inaugural Address, setting forth an extreme left-wing political program. By this time British trade unions were permitted by law, and were beginning to exert considerable influence on industrial relations. The leaders were eager to improve working-class conditions; but they boycotted the First International because, while they favored reform, most were opposed to outright revolution. Many socialist groups in the continental countries refused to attend the meetings for the same reason.

As a result the First International made little impact on European socialism and in the early 1870's it foundered. The organization had been weakened by fierce clashes of opinion between Karl Marx, a Russian anarchist named Mikhail Bakunin, and the French advocate of social reform Pierre Proudhon. Bakunin, the son of a prosperous landowner, had turned against his own class and become a violent atheist and ruthless anarchist, determined to abolish religious belief and do away with all existing forms of government. He was an agitator rather than a philosopher, aspiring to lead a group of international revolutionaries. Proudhon proposed economic reform through the mutual association of employers and workers. He did not favor the abolition of capitalism, nor did he advocate common ownership; and Marx had always considered his projects both impractical and harmful to the cause of socialism.

Marx's most famous written work is *Das Kapital (Capital)*. In these three massive volumes he presented a detailed record of his deliberations and ultimate conclusions. The first volume of *Das Kapital* was published in German in 1867, and in an English edition in 1899. The second and third volumes appeared soon after Marx's death, but owing to the difficulties of translation they were not published in English until 1907 and 1909 respectively. Since that time the entire work has been translated into more than thirty languages. Marx has been acknowledged as the greatest authority on world socialism and *Das Kapital* has been accepted as the Bible of communism.

In this vast collection of historical, scientific and economic data, the result of long years of research, there are obvious instances of contradiction and doubt. Marx himself had always stressed the absolute necessity of modifying laws and opinions to fit varying circumstances, and many of his treasured expectations have indeed not come to pass. Though he prided himself on being a realist, some of his theories were too idealistic, or even utopian, for everyday life.

In 1883 Karl Marx died in a shabby London boarding house. He had been very lonely since his wife's death fifteen months earlier. He was worn out by persistent poverty, weakened by ill health, and exhausted by the magnitude of his self-appointed task. He was buried in Highgate Cemetery in North London beside his wife, who had shared the privations of an outcast revolutionary with steadfast love and loyalty. In a speech at Marx's graveside Engels paid a last tribute to his friend. He said: "As Darwin discovered the law of development of organic nature, so Marx discovered the law of the development of human history."

5 · Bismarck Speeds the Birth of Bolshevism

WHILE MARX WAS WORKING in London, in Germany disillusionment and domestic dissension followed the failure of the Frankfurt Parliament. During these troubled years Otto von Bismarck, the son of a Junker (noble) landowner, was working his way to the very forefront of Prussian politics. He became first Premier of Prussia and later Chancellor of the German Empire. Trained originally as a lawyer, Bismarck had entered government judicial service and then turned to politics. He soon made his name as a die-hard conservative, opposed to socialism, liberalism, or any kind of parliamentary reform. He had a brilliant mind, a compelling personality and an iron will. He also had unshakeable faith in the glorious destiny of his country and was determined that nothing should stand in the way of Prussian leadership of the German states.

By shrewd diplomacy, backed up by force of arms, Bismarck defeated first Denmark, then Austria and finally France. He had no scruples when it came to furthering the interests of Prussia and he managed to make it appear that both Austria and France were the real aggressors in each war. Both countries were overwhelmed by the speed and firepower of the Prussian armies.

In January 1871, after a disastrous siege, Paris surrendered and Bismarck was triumphant. There remained no Continental power strong enough to hinder his great ambition. In the magnificent Hall of Mirrors in the Palace of Versailles, the scene of former French grandeur, William I, King of Prussia, was proclaimed Emperor of Germany. Many German-speaking states which had not already joined the victorious Prussians hastened to do so. Together they formed the first German Empire and took from France the rich province of Alsace-Lorraine—an act which created bitter resentment among patriotic Frenchmen. Austria was the only German-speaking country which did not apply for admission to the empire. Humiliated by Prussian defeat, the Austrians preferred to be independent. This was precisely what Bismarck had planned, for he saw clearly that Prussia and Austria could never peacefully share the same crown. He himself took the post of chancellor, with unlimited powers. William I was emperor in name, but Bismarck held the reins of government.

In the second half of the nineteenth century the Germans made enormous industrial progress. They took up English inventions and adapted them to their own needs. Under the direction of talented engineers, chemists and scientists, production soared. The Ruhr region northeast of the Rhine River is rich in coal. Mines and foundries, steel works and shipyards, laboratories and factories increased each year. In the Ruhr town of Essen, in 1810, an enterprising blacksmith named Friedrich Krupp started a small iron foundry which, during the next sixty years, grew into the largest armament factory in the world. When William

II was crowned Emperor of Germany in 1888 he inherited an immensely powerful war machine.

The German Empire had become an important world power, but rapid industrial expansion created social problems at home. Peasants left the mountains, the forests and the farmland to find better-paying work in the towns. Many were exploited by unscrupulous employers, but the industrial conditions in Germany were never as bad as those in England. The peasants kept a closer connection between town and country life; factory workers returned to their villages for religious festivals and family occasions. If they were out of work they made their way home and were seldom destitute.

But Bismarck was not prepared to leave social welfare to chance or to the action of socialist reformers. He saw that if Germany was going to become a rich industrial power, he must win the loyalty of the workers, arouse their patriotism, and make them proud to be citizens of a mighty empire. They must realize that they owed their well-being solely to the generosity of the state. He introduced national insurance for accidents, sickness and old age, and made sure that no political party but his own could take the credit.

While Bismarck was building an empire and arming it against external attack, Marx was building a political movement to destroy Germany, and other such capitalist states, from within. In England, the land of his exile, circumstances were very different from those in Germany, the land of his birth. While Marx was working on *Das Kapital,* Englishmen enjoyed freedom of speech and they were not punished for expressing their political views. Although the working class did not yet have the right to vote, people were permitted their own opinions and they could air them in Parliament, in pubs or at street corners. Writers and speakers were not imprisoned or banished for grumbling about the government, and Marx published *Das Kapital* openly without fear of reprisal.

In Germany, under the stern direction of Bismarck, soon known as "The Iron Chancellor," the people did not have the same degree of freedom. It was unwise to question a government decree and dangerous to possess a copy of the *Communist Manifesto*. The followers of Karl Marx and Hegel had formed a political party and called themselves Social Democrats. From the day Bismarck came to power he distrusted them, labeled them "the social peril," and waited for an opportunity to suppress them. He grasped at the attempted assassination of the emperor —by a fanatic Bismarck claimed was a Social Democrat—as an excuse to declare the party illegal, ban its press, and forbid all meetings. From this time onward the Social Democrats became an underground movement, operated by a small but fanatical band of Marx's disciples. They held their meetings in secret, set up clandestine printing presses, and produced socialist tracts in German, French, Italian and, most important of all, Russian, for Marx had taught them that the czarist regime was the ultimate expression of capitalist tyranny.

While western Europe was making rapid advances in scientific knowledge and industrial development, Russia remained a feudal society with an economy based on serf labor. The word of the czar was law and the people had no voice in the government. Although the Russian nobles and landowners denounced the principles behind the French Revolution of 1789, peasant soldiers who had fought in the Napoleonic Wars had brought back reports of greater political freedom and fairer land distribution abroad and had stimulated discontent at home.

In 1855 Alexander II, the descendant of a long line of Romanov rulers, came to the Russian throne. He was a kindly, well-meaning monarch, with an honest desire to improve the lot of his people. He saw the injustice of serfdom and resolved to abolish it. In 1861, by imperial decree, he emancipated the serfs throughout the whole of Russia. But, although the peasants were legally free from bondage, they were still chained by poverty. They had expected to receive land as a gift; but they soon found that they were liable for rent and also, if they wanted to own a plot, they had to make payments for forty-nine years, and very few of them could raise the money.

However, Alexander followed up the liberation of the serfs by appointing county councils, or *zemstva,* to organize public services. He reformed the law courts and reduced the peasants' heavy burden of active military service from twenty-five to sixteen years, making it compulsory for all classes of society. In the reign of Alexander II industry expanded and communications improved, but Russia was still far behind her western neighbors. Although in the first wave of enthusiasm he was hailed as "the czar liberator," Alexander's reforms came too late and gave too little to wipe out former grievances.

Revolutionary doctrines began to penetrate all levels of Russian thought, and a revolutionary movement took shape in the newly formed middle class, the Russian bourgeoisie. By the second half of the nineteenth century a smattering of Russian students were studying at universities in Germany and Switzerland. Many of them were girls, for there were no universities for women in Russia. Free discussion was also limited in Germany, but many young intellectuals joined secret societies and were attracted by socialist doctrines. They looked forward to the prospect of equality as an outcome of class warfare and carried new ideas back to their home cities, towns and villages. Writers and professors gathered groups of students to discuss literature, which was permitted by Russian law; and politics, which was strictly forbidden.

From these discussions there gradually emerged a number of different revolutionary groups. Some followed the teaching of Marx and Engels. Others agreed with the opinions of the Russian philosophers Alexander Herzen and Peter Lavrov, who hoped for the development of socialism through the betterment of existing conditions and a clear understanding of the aims and possibilities of reform. But many young revolutionaries were inflamed by the anarchist Mikhail Bakunin who told them not to waste time studying learned theories, but to go straight to the peasants and spur them on to revolt. These youthful idealists later took the name of Populists, but their expeditions to arouse the villagers were not a great success. The peasants were poor, but they were also very conservative and, at heart, loyal to the czar—their "little father." They regarded these townspeople—who arrived often in peasant costume—with the utmost resentment and distrust.

In 1866 a band of students plotted to kill the Czar. The attempt was unsuccessful but Alexander grew very wary. He dismissed some of his liberal advisers and slowed down his reforms. In 1876 a secret society was founded, under the name Land and Liberty, to stir up rebellion. It was broken up by the police, the leaders were imprisoned, and the society disbanded. In 1879 the most extreme members of the group who had managed to escape capture formed a terrorist party which they called The People's Will. They were not Marxists, for although they planned to divide the land among the peasants, they also visualized a national government to give the people the rule of their own choosing.

But the leaders of The People's Will believed that their first and most important mission was to assassinate the Czar, and that nothing could be accomplished until he was dead. Therefore they took to terrorism as a means to an end. They blew up the imperial train and concealed a time bomb in the banquet hall of the Winter Palace. By chance the Czar escaped death on both occasions. In March 1881, after great misgivings, he signed a document giving elected representatives of the people the right to sit on state advisory councils. On the same day he attended a military parade. As he drove back to the palace in an open carriage, one of his Cossack guards was wounded by a bomb intended for the Czar. Careless of his own safety, Alexander stopped the carriage and stepped down to help the injured man. He was killed by a second bomb thrown, like the first, by a member of The People's Will.

A wave of anger and fear followed the crime and Alexander

The assassination of Czar Alexander II, 1881

III, who succeeded his father, used his authority to stamp out any movement leading to reform, or any indication of independent thought or action. An army of secret police rounded up revolutionaries and reformers alike. A period of harsh restraint settled over Russia and all the good will which might have followed Alexander's well-intentioned concessions was lost in a burst of hatred and revenge.

Meanwhile socialism in Germany gained inner strength through outward repression; and Bismarck's ban on liberal reformers merely served to heighten the sense of purpose and harden the resolve of the Social Democrats. Danger added fire to revolutionary zeal. As a result Germany became the secret source of a stream of propaganda seeping into Russia.

At the same time, dedicated Russian revolutionaries set up headquarters abroad and prepared for the day when the proletariat would come into its own. In the Bavarian city of Munich a highly organized group of Russian conspirators worked with a branch of the secret Social Democratic Party. One leader of the group was a middle-aged exile of noble family, Georgy Plekhanov, known to later historians as "the father of Russian Marxism." Another was a young Russian revolutionary who later became world famous under the assumed name of Lenin.

The execution of the Czar's assassins

Plekhanov was the first Russian to expound the philosophy of Marxism. He had a profound effect on the rise of socialism and on the development of Lenin. Later the two men differed, for Plekhanov was more moderate in his attitude to social and constitutional change; but in these early days, Lenin held the older socialist in great respect.

From a carefully concealed printing press in Leipzig, they rolled off socialist literature and in 1900 published the first edition of a revolutionary journal symbolically entitled *Iskra,* or *The Spark,* because it aimed to fire the imagination of all who suffered from poverty and oppression.

The publication and distribution of *Iskra* was conducted with the courage and precision of a military operation. It was printed in minute type on thin, onionskin paper. Then the *Iskra* staff folded the leaves into flat slips, concealed them in cargoes of non-contraband goods, and transported the cases to prearranged meeting places close to the Russian border. At these secret junctions the packages were handed over to professional smugglers who, despite the precautions of the frontier guards, carried them into Russia and delivered them to a chain of socialist agents. In spite of the vigilance of the Russian police force and the certain knowledge that any messenger caught with revolutionary material would be shot as a traitor, cast into a czarist prison, or banished to hard labor in Siberia, waiting committees all over the country got their deliveries of *Iskra* and filtered them into the factories. Sometimes copies of *Iskra* fluttered down like a cloud of autumn leaves from the gallery of a darkened theater. In the opening years of the twentieth century thousands of educated Russians were familiar with the teachings of Karl Marx and were in sympathy with the revolutionary movement. And little by little the proletariat was introduced to the image of socialism.

In 1902 the editors of *Iskra* moved to London. There Lenin met for the first time a dashing young Jewish revolutionary who had just escaped from Siberia and was traveling with a false passport in the conspirator's name of Trotsky. From that day until Lenin's death in 1924, Lenin and Trotsky were almost constantly in touch with one another. Although they differed at times in their interpretation of Marxist doctrine, they were both utterly devoted to the communist cause, and in the most critical hours of the Bolshevik Revolution they held the fate of Russia in their hands.

6 · *The Road to Revolution*

IN 1870 VLADIMIR ULYANOV, the founder of Russian communism, was born in a respectable middle-class home in a small provincial town on the banks of the Volga River. His father was a teacher and school administrator, his mother a doctor's daughter, and they were a devoted family. Vladimir was the third of six children and he had a happy childhood. When he was sixteen, his older brother Alexander was executed in St. Petersburg for taking part in a plot to kill Alexander III, the reigning czar. Vladimir had always looked up to his brother as a hero and it is said that in that year he swore to avenge his death. All the Ulyanov children had been brought up in the teaching of the Russian Orthodox Church, but Vladimir stated in later life that in the year his brother died "he perceived clearly that there was no God."

After the execution, the Ulyanov family was put on a police black list, suspected of anti-czarist activities, and Vladimir was expelled from Kazan University for taking part in a student demonstration. However he eventually graduated in law with top honors at St. Petersburg. By this time he had been reading the writings of Karl Marx for five years and was an authority on

The Ulyanov family, Vladimir is seated at bottom right

Marxist doctrine. He soon set out to educate factory groups in the theory behind the *Communist Manifesto*. He also traveled to Switzerland, France and Germany to make contact with the chief revolutionary exiles and widen his field of knowledge. Most conspirators changed their names to escape police identification and soon the world knew Vladimir Ulyanov as Lenin. In political and philosophical discussions he proved himself not only intelligent, but also practical. It was not long before he became an acknowledged leader in the Russian revolutionary movement.

In 1895 Lenin returned to Russia carrying a supply of contraband literature hidden in a suitcase especially fitted with a false bottom. By this time the police regarded him as a dangerous conspirator. They trailed his every movement, but for some months he escaped them. Finally an accomplice betrayed him and he was first imprisoned in the St. Petersburg jail and then sent to Siberia for three years. During his exile Lenin married Nadezhda Konstantinovna Krupskaya, a fellow conspirator who followed him to Siberia. She served with him loyally in the revolutionary cause and, for the rest of his life, tried to shield him from danger and repair the damage of overwork and nervous strain.

In 1894 Nicholas II, the last of the Romanovs, came to the Russian throne. He inherited a country in urgent need of constitutional reform, and ripe for revolution. He was tragically unfitted for the difficult role he had to play, entirely lacking in political wisdom, and with no concept of the gigantic problems which threatened to engulf him. Nicholas was an autocrat, successor to a long line of imperious rulers. But he was also a shy and retiring man. He married a young Hessian princess who was as unrealistic as he was. In 1904, after four daughters, Alexis, the longed-for heir to the throne, was born. To the grief of his parents, the boy had inherited hemophilia from his mother—a blood disease in which the slightest injury can cause fatal bleeding. In their anxiety for the child, the parents consulted first the best doctors they could find and then, as there was no medical cure, they turned to all kinds of faith healers. Finally the Empress fell under the spell of Gregory Rasputin, an uneducated Siberian peasant who claimed to be a monk. Rasputin had gained an evil reputation for his dissolute behavior. He boasted of divine power to help Alexis, and while he was at court the little boy survived several crises. Because of the devotion of the Empress, Rasputin became very powerful, and this sinister association sharpened the indignation of Russian people of all classes against their rulers.

In 1898 Russian socialists formed an official Social Democratic Party. Lenin was then in exile and he had become a hardened revolutionary, experienced in conspiracy, sobered by arrest and imprisonment. When differences of opinion arose among the Social Democrats he led the faction later known as the Bolsheviks, from the Russian word *bolshinstvo,* meaning majority. He was determined to bring about the downfall of the czarist-capitalist regime and build a proletarian paradise out of the ruins. The other Social Democratic faction was known as the Mensheviks, from the Russian word *menshinstvo,* meaning minority. The chief aim of this group was to get possession of the land and divide it among the peasants. They differed from Lenin because they were prepared to establish democratic government through constitutional reform, whereas he would contemplate only total revolution. Later, the Mensheviks broke away from the Social Democrats and formed the Social Revolutionary Party.

When Lenin first published *Iskra* he was only thirty years old, but in a strange way he did not belong to any age group. He had set himself a lifework so early that both mentally and physically youth seemed to have passed him by. He began losing his hair at twenty and by thirty he was almost bald. He was rather short and thickset, with blunt features, pale skin and red hair. His appearance would have been somewhat insignificant had it not been for his piercing gray eyes, and his dynamic fund of nervous energy.

Lenin became the leader of the revolutionary movement though an unshakeable sense of personal mission, an immense capacity for hard work, a genius for organization, a passionate faith in Marxist theory, and a lack of pity for those who failed in an appointed task. Older socialists, like Plekhanov, recognized his usefulness to the cause. In 1902 Lenin's pamphlet "What is to be done?" was accepted as the blueprint for party policy. The pamphlet began with an attack on all those who believed that trade unions were the best means of helping the working class to improve its position in the world. Marx acknowledged that trade unions were formed to fight the bosses, but the very need for their existence emphasized the fact that the workers were slaves of the bourgeoisie. Lenin drew a sharp line between the party intellectuals, or professional revolutionaries, and the mass of the workers who made up the proletariat and were uneducated in politics. He laid down what proved to be the main law of a revolutionary party: absolute obedience to the communist elite. The rank and file of party members must accept unquestioningly the directives of the professional revolutionaries. They must never be satisfied with anything less than permanent agitation. They must despise not only trade union treaties but also all government reforms, and regard them as infantile, make-believe playing at politics compared to the reality of revolutionary communism.

In 1904 Czar Nicholas—hoping to enlarge his empire, gain popularity by an easy victory and avert revolution—committed Russia to a war with Japan. Neither he nor his ministers had any idea of Japanese preparedness and efficiency or of the widespread corruption among Russian military contractors at home. The poorly equipped Russian forces suffered humiliating defeats on land and sea, and bad news from the Far Eastern front added to the tension at home.

In January 1905 an unforeseen disaster occurred. Thousands of workmen, members of a newly formed Union of Russian Workers, and led by a priest named Gregory Gapon, marched through the streets of St. Petersburg to the Winter Palace to present petitions for better living conditions to their czar. Their wives and children marched with them. They sang religious songs and carried banners, but no arms. The Czar was absent and the palace guard, in a moment of panic, fired on the defenseless crowd. Hundreds of people were killed and many more injured.

The massacre of Bloody Sunday, January 9, 1905

The news of "Bloody Sunday" roused the whole country to anger and protest. Riots and strikes broke out and the revolutionary spirit spread to the armed forces. The soldiers of the czar refused to obey their officers and fire on the rioters. In June the sailors of the great battleship *Potemkin*, the finest ship in the Russian Navy, shot their officers and raised the red flag at the masthead. In October St. Petersburg was paralyzed by a general strike.

In the same month the Constitutional Democratic Party (Kadet) was formed. Its members were liberal and left wing but not revolutionary. The Kadet party policy was to elect first a

representative assembly and then establish a national government, or *duma,* to run the country along democratic lines. The
Czar was torn by doubt and indecision. He threatened to abdicate but his ministers dissuaded him. Finally he agreed to convene
a national duma, a parliament of freely elected members; promised to make laws guaranteeing personal freedom; and granted
an amnesty, or pardon, to all political prisoners and exiles.

In the confusion which followed the massacre on Bloody
Sunday, a group of Mensheviks set up headquarters in St. Petersburg under the leadership of Trotsky, who had returned to Russia
and managed to escape arrest. The Mensheviks formed a *soviet,*
or council, issued strike orders, and preached permanent revolution. They called themselves the Soviet Council of Workers'
Deputies and were a force to be reckoned with. For the first time
in Russian history, the working class openly exerted political
power.

News of Bloody Sunday reached Lenin in Geneva. He believed that full-scale revolution would follow immediately and
that the time was ripe for the dictatorship of the proletariat. He
went to London, rallied the exiled Social Democrats, set about
organizing a revolutionary army and raising money to smuggle
arms into Russia. But when he arrived in St. Petersburg in November 1905, after the amnesty, he found the Soviet in the hands
of the Mensheviks, and the Kadets gaining popular support in
their efforts to compromise with the Czar and establish a constitutional parliament. Although the country was riddled with
revolutionary ideas, there were few Social Democrats working
along pure Marxist lines.

In the following month the Czar ordered the arrest of the entire St. Petersburg Soviet, including Trotsky. In reprisal, workers in Moscow staged an armed uprising. The Czar sent in his crack regiment, the Semenov Guards, to disperse the rebels. They carried out their orders with ruthless severity and the forces of revolution were temporarily subdued. But later Lenin spoke of the Moscow uprising as a dress rehearsal for the revolution of 1917.

In the spring of 1906 the promised Duma met, but the Czar's opening proclamation made it clear that he had curtailed its powers. Therefore the Duma fell far short of the demands and expectations of the liberal politicians who were seeking representational government. After two and a half months of troubled existence it petered out. Lenin had consistently denounced this Duma as an utter fraud and forbidden the Bolsheviks to take any part in the elections. In subsequent elections Lenin changed his tactics and encouraged Bolsheviks to run as candidates for the Duma. They entered parliament, not to represent their constituents, but to spread Marxist propaganda from a parliamentary platform.

During the next eight years successive Dumas introduced a number of long overdue reforms. By 1914 one peasant in every four owned his land and about half the children of school age had some education. Though these Dumas were not truly democratic, they were at least national assemblies and the majority of Russians preferred legal government to armed rebellion. For the time being revolutionary doctrines were out of favor.

Lenin spent most of these years in Finland, traveling from time to time to Sweden, England, France, Austria and Switzerland to conspire with leading Social Democrats. It was for him a period of acute disappointment and bitter frustration. Western Europe was prosperous and at peace, and the chances of a proletarian uprising were remote. At a Social Democratic congress in London, Lenin had won control of the Central Committee of the Bolshevik Party, but he was constantly up against Menshevik opposition and he urgently needed money to finance propaganda and prepare key centers in Russia for future action. He collected donations from Maxim Gorky, the famous writer, and other wealthy Russian socialists. But most of the Bolshevik Party funds came from bank raids and armed holdups. In carefully planned robberies, gangs of Bolshevik bandits seized hundreds of thousands of rubles for the cause.

In 1914 this comparative peace and social progress was shattered by the outbreak of the First World War. Since the founding of the German Empire, tension in Europe had been rising. Germany and Britain were engaged in an arms race and both nations had constructed impressive fleets of warships. But in an age of empire-building, Britain had outpaced Germany in overseas conquest, and national rivalry had reached a dangerous peak.

In June 1914 the Archduke Franz Ferdinand, heir to the Austrian throne, was assassinated by a political fanatic in Sarejevo, the capital of Serbia—a small Balkan country which is now part of Yugoslavia, but was then part of the Austro-Hungarian Empire. Because a number of European heads of state harbored ambitions that could only be realized by armed force, this isolated incident sparked off a world conflagration.

Franz Joseph, the aged Austrian Emperor, declared war on

Serbia to avenge the murder and to establish Austrian rule in the Balkans. William II, Emperor of Germany, supported Austria and attacked Belgium knowing that Britain had treaty obligations which would bring her to Belgium's aid. William hoped to defeat Britain at sea and seize her colonies. The French were prepared to fight Germany to wipe out the shame of 1870 and win back Alsace-Lorraine. And Czar Nicholas II of Russia, who had treaty obligations to France and England, saw in a Balkan war a chance of diverting the attention of the Russian people from internal troubles by the capture of Constantinople from the Turks. For centuries Russian rulers, in their landlocked country, had coveted this great warm-water port as a center of trade and a status symbol among nations.

Therefore in the summer of 1914 Russia joined the allied forces of Great Britain and the Dominions, France, Belgium and Serbia—later to be strengthened by the forces of the United States, Italy and Japan—in armed combat against Germany, the Austro-Hungarian Empire, Turkey and Bulgaria.

At the beginning of the war, Russians of all classes were united by a great surge of patriotic feeling. As an expression of national pride Nicholas changed the name of his capital from the German St. Petersburg to the Russian Petrograd. Able-bodied peasants were called up and hurriedly sent off to the front. Most went to war willingly, for they believed that if they fought bravely for their czar and returned victorious they would then be rewarded with land of their own. At home old men, women and children took over the work in the fields, but they could not produce enough crops to feed the people in the cities. Bread lines grew longer and longer and often housewives went home empty-handed. The Russian armies were no match for the Germans. The soldiers were neither as well armed nor trained; and although they fought gallantly, they were driven back with heavy losses. News of the casualties deepened the despair on the home front.

In September 1915 liberal members of the Duma begged the Czar to authorize an emergency coalition government, composed of representatives of all parties, to review the conduct of the war and handle the desperate food situation. Backed by the Empress and irresponsible ministers, Nicholas replied by dismissing every man in the Duma who favored coalition. By this ill-advised action he sealed his doom, for the Duma lost the confidence of the people and could no longer lead public opinion toward moderation.

At this time the Czar made a final error. He discharged the Grand Duke Nicholas, who was an experienced soldier, and appointed himself commander-in-chief of the Russian armies. Then, in order to raise the morale of his troops, he left Petrograd and moved to the supreme army headquarters at the Ukrainian town of Mogilev, five hundred miles from the capital, leaving the government in the hands of the Empress. She never made a decision without consulting Rasputin, until 1916 when Prince Yusupov and a small group of men, members of noble Russian families, murdered the faith healer in a vain attempt to save the monarchy.

In March 1917 events reached a climax. The commander of the Petrograd garrison wired the Czar that there were uprisings in the city; the troops were mutinous and the workers were strik-

Czar Nicholas II with the Czarevitch Alexis, 1911

ing for food. Nicholas simply replied: "Stop the disorder in the capital at once." Princes, grand dukes, statesmen and foreign diplomats implored the Czar to make concessions to stave off total disaster, but he took no notice. His only action was to dissolve the remainder of the Duma, thus destroying the last defense of the monarchy against revolution.

Finally, in response to urgent entreaty, he ordered the imperial train and set out for Petrograd. By this time the people were completely out of hand. Even the Czar's own bodyguard had deserted their posts and joined the revolutionary mobs milling through the streets. It was too late to hope that Nicholas could restore order.

Meanwhile revolutionary socialist groups had formed a soviet on the lines of the St. Petersburg Soviet of 1905, under the name of the Soviet of Workers' and Soldiers' Deputies. In the same week the Duma, which had refused to disperse, met to appoint a provisional government headed by Prince Lvov, a liberal nobleman, to take temporary charge of the situation. People of all shades of political opinion agreed that the Czar should abdicate. Early on the morning on March 15, 1917, two deputies left Petrograd to intercept Nicholas on his journey. They bore a document of abdication for the Czar's signature. The same evening they reached the imperial train at the town of Pskov, near the Estonian frontier. Nicholas had already made his decision. He signed the act of abdication calmly and without delay. After three hundred years of imperial rule, the Romanov dynasty was at an end.

This stage of the Russian Revolution was carried out with

little bloodshed. The movement for democratic government had originated mainly among the bourgeoisie, but under pressure of war it spread to all ranks of society. The Czar was overthrown by general consent and national necessity.

But freedom was shortlived for the Russian people. The bourgeois revolution had destroyed an ancient dictatorship; the Bolshevik revolution was about to create a new one.

7 · *Lenin Comes to Power*

ONE OF THE FIRST ACTIONS of the Provisional Government in Petrograd was to grant an amnesty to everyone who had been imprisoned or exiled for political offenses during the czarist regime. At the same time it announced freedom of the press and of speech, and promised to organize elections for a Constituent Assembly so that the Russian people could decide for themselves the form of permanent government they wanted. To many Russians it seemed that at long last the dreams of democracy were coming true.

News of the amnesty traveled far and fast. Political prisoners were released from prisons all over Russia and from labor camps in Siberia. Exiles set out from points of refuge in Europe, the United States and Canada, and flocked to Petrograd. At the height of the First World War travelers were restricted by battles on land, and menaced by submarine attacks at sea, but the repatriates were not deterred. They reached Russia by devious routes, determined to take part in this new freedom.

When Lenin first received the sensational reports of the revolution and abdication he was in Switzerland, hemmed in between opposing armies—the Germans on the east and the French and British on the west. He had welcomed the war as an opportunity to overthrow the capitalist system and promote world socialism, but the rapid turn of events in Russia took him by surprise. He felt isolated from politics and was frantic to get home and take over direct control of the Bolshevik Party.

There was, at this time, a division of opinion among European socialists. Many of them in peacetime had called themselves "internationalists," holding the ideal of a stateless society. But when it came to actual war most of them had decided to bury political differences with their own governments and present a united front to the enemy.

Lenin however remained true to Marxist aims. He was confident that when a revolution broke out, no matter in what country, it would sweep through Europe and national loyalties would fade away. He regarded the Russian armies, commanded by men of the officer class, as a relic of czarism, and he had no qualms about undermining army discipline. He was not appalled by the prospect of a German victory because he was so sure that in the workers' world after the war no one nation would dominate another. In 1915 at a congress of European Social Democrats in Switzerland he tried unsuccessfully to launch a manifesto calling on the workers of all the warring countries to put away their tools, and the soldiers to lay down their arms. The motion was defeated by socialists who considered patriotism even more important than politics.

When Lenin applied to the French and British authorities for a travel permit to return to Russia they refused the request.

The Russian armies were already cracking, and it was clear that when Lenin reached Petrograd he would do everything within his power to bring about their total collapse. The Germans on the other hand were only too glad to send an agitator into Russia to sabotage their enemy's war effort. They hoped to conclude a peace with Russia and transfer whole divisions from the eastern front to smash the French and British armies in the west.

So the German Government arranged for Lenin, his wife and a group of fellow exiles to pass through Germany in a sealed railway carriage under armed guard. Late in the evening of April 16, 1917, the party arrived in Petrograd. They were greeted rapturously by a crowd of revolutionaries singing the "Marseillaise" and waving red flags. It was a historic moment, but few onlookers who saw Vladimir Ulyanov, alias Lenin—a small middle-aged man in a shabby jacket and workman's cap, awkwardly clasping a presentation bouquet of flowers—would have predicted that in less than a year he would be supreme master of all Russia.

On the same evening Lenin made a speech. He assured his Bolshevik audience that socialist revolutions were also beginning in England, Germany and France; that the "toiling masses" were about to come into their own. He predicted that in Russia the period of bourgeois rule was drawing to a close and the proletarian revolution was near at hand. A few days later he published his famous revolutionary *Theses* in the Bolshevik newspaper *Pravda,* calling for civil war in Russia to establish a classless society, and to end conflict between nations.

Lenin's arrival was reported in all the Petrograd news-

Lenin addresses the workers

papers, but his name was little known except to professional revolutionaries, and few people took much notice of his pronouncements. His main strength lay in the weakness of his political opponents. Since the March Revolution there had been two forms of government in Petrograd competing for power. The first was the Provisional Government, heir to the Duma, composed mainly of middle-class liberal and moderate socialist members, with a smattering of the nobility; and the second was the Soviet of Workers' and Soldiers' Deputies, under Menshevik leadership and representing the interests of the factory workers backed up by the rank and file of the army. Now that the first excitement had died down, the people found that despite the liberation from czarist rule, they were still hungry. Neither government was sufficiently strong to take charge of the situation and improve the food supply, so little was done. But the Provisional Government and the Petrograd Soviet had one common policy, for all their members were determined to carry on the fight against Germany until they could make peace without loss of territory or self-respect. The Bolsheviks had very little support and no representatives in either government. But Lenin forbade his followers to collaborate with any other political group of the Social Democratic Party. For the first time he suggested dropping the name Social Democrat and adopting the term Communist.

The Petrograd Soviet had become the center of a chain of soviets, or local councils, linking the workers in towns and cities throughout Russia. Lenin coined the fighting slogan: "All power to the Soviets." He saw that, at this stage, he was far too weak to challenge the Soviets' authority, and it was therefore politic

Voting in a local Soviet

to give them outward support and gain a foothold among the workers. At the same time he undermined the popularity of the Mensheviks by spreading propaganda pamphlets promising "land, peace and bread" when the Bolsheviks came to power.

Alexander Kerensky, a prominent Menshevik, had become Minister for War at the formation of the Provisional Government. On June 29, 1917, he called for a grand offensive on the southwestern sector of the battle front, hoping to show the French and British that the Russians had no intention of making a separate peace with Germany, and also to raise the fighting spirit of the Russian armies. On July 1, the Russians struck and made some impressive gains until the Germans brought in fresh reserves, drove back the exhausted and ill-fed peasant army and inflicted fearful losses.

Lenin had sent agents out to the villages to fill the land-hungry people with false hopes of Bolshevik bounty, and to the fighting lines to persuade soldiers who were discouraged by reverses and tired of the war to defy their officers, pack up their guns, go home to their families and seize land. Many joined the Bolshevik Party simply because they saw in a second revolution a possible end to their hardship and suffering.

Meanwhile in Petrograd Lenin and his comrades were inciting rebellion. In mid-July the Soviets of Workers' and Soldiers' Deputies of all Russia were holding a congress in the capital. The Bolsheviks secretly organized a mass march of their supporters,

The Petrograd uprising, July 1917

starting as a demonstration against inefficient government and developing into an armed insurrection. Lenin had arranged for the march to take place during the Congress so that the Bolsheviks could come into the open with dramatic force, declaring themselves champions of the poor to Soviet delegates from all over Russia. The workers set out according to plan, marching through the streets of Petrograd to the strains of the "Internationale," the revolutionary song which had succeeded the "Marseillaise" as a battle anthem. But before the shooting began, Lenin backed down. He suddenly decided that it was too early to show his hand. He ordered the Bolshevik organizers to keep out of the way and afterward denied all knowledge of the origin of the disorders which did occur. But the police were warned; they put out a warrant for Lenin's arrest, and he fled from the country to seek shelter in Finland. He crossed the frontier disguised as a laborer and for two weeks he and a fellow Bolshevik lay concealed in a hollowed-out haystack. Later he found an ideal refuge in the house of a Finnish head of police who happened also to be a Bolshevik.

The prestige of the Provisional Government declined sharply after the disastrous June offensive against the German Army. On July 21 Prince Lvov resigned and Kerensky succeeded him as Premier. At the time of the March Revolution Kerensky had been a national hero, an ardent patriot and an outright advocate of parliamentary reform. As a Menshevik he held official positions both in the Petrograd Soviet and the Provisional Government, but his actions were hampered by the rivalry between the two. As Minister for War he was held responsible for the recent military failure and his popularity waned.

In the summer of 1917 Kerensky appointed a new Commander-in-Chief of the Russian armies, General Kornilov. It was an unfortunate choice. Kornilov was brave in battle but entirely ignorant of politics. One of his comrades remarked that he had "the heart of a lion, and the brains of a lamb." He pictured himself as the savior of Russia, chosen by fate to stamp out the evil influences which were demoralizing the army. Kornilov decided to purify the administration by suppressing the Soviet of Workers' and Soldiers' Deputies and the Bolshevik agitators in Petrograd once and for all. He led a force against the city and the enraged workers rose in a body to repulse the approaching invaders. Kornilov's troops were confused and uncertain. They did not want to fight their own people and they fell apart before they ever reached Petrograd. The Kornilov affair did irreparable harm to the Provisional Government, and the only people who benefited were the workers who seized arms to defend the capital and kept them when the threat of invasion was passed. They later formed the first units of the Red Guard, the hard core of Lenin's army.

From his hideout in Finland, Lenin directed a destructive campaign against the Provisional Government. He issued orders which were faithfully carried out by Trotsky, his second in command. Trotsky was a brilliant orator and a man of action, able and intelligent. On October 8 he became chairman of the Petrograd Soviet. For the first time a Bolshevik was officially appointed to high office, and many of the Party felt that they were making political progress and would gain the positions they wanted without resorting to force. But Lenin refused to consider any plan for attaining power by peaceful means, for Marx had said repeatedly that the new proletarian state could only arise from the ruins of the old. The Provisional Government fixed the date for the elections of a Constituent Assembly for November 25. Lenin knew that the Bolsheviks had no chance of winning an open election. He had to avoid, at any cost, a public demonstration of Bolshevik weakness. So he determined to stage an armed uprising before the country had a chance to vote. In October, under Trotsky's leadership, the Petrograd Soviet created the main arm of Bolshevik assault, the Military Revolutionary Committee.

On October 3, although notices were still out for his arrest, Lenin returned to Petrograd disguised behind a false wig and a bandaged face. His comrades warned him of the danger but they could not keep him away. Many of them still favored a people's election and opposed armed force. At a stormy all-night session of the Bolshevik Central Committee, Lenin finally got his way. The official figures were ten in favor of all-out insurrection, and two against.

According to Lenin the uprising had to be organized "in a Marxist way," that is: "as an art, we must, without losing a single moment, organize a general staff of the insurrectionary detachments, we must distribute our forces, . . . we must mobilize the workers and call upon them to engage in a last desperate fight. . . ."

November 7, 1917, was fixed as the vital day, the moment for decisive action. Revolutionary headquarters were set up in the grim Petrograd fortress of St. Peter and St. Paul. The Bolsheviks planned the operation with meticulous care. Before dawn, armed detachments of Red Guards occupied all the key points in the city. They took over the power stations, post offices, telephone exchanges, and many government buildings. They placed guards on the bridges and at railway stations. Some of the population was pro-Bolshevik, others were dazed. There was little resistance and no shooting. The Provisional Government assembled at the Winter Palace, the former residence of the czar. Almost the only troops who had remained loyal were young officer cadets, still in the course of their training. Every member of the Provisional Government knew that the guns of the cruiser *Aurora,* anchored in the nearby Neva River, were manned by Bolshevik sailors and trained on the Winter Palace. Gradually the Bolshevik forces moved through the city and closed in with field guns and armored cars. But as they forced their way through the palace gates, they were disarmed by the defenders. Evening came and the revolutionary command issued an ultimatum demanding surrender by eight o'clock. The Provisional Government made no move. The Bolsheviks gave them an hour's grace but soon after nine o'clock a shell from the *Aurora* exploded with a blinding crash in the palace yard. In the subsequent confusion Red Guards entered the palace and made their way through the maze of corridors to the cabinet room where the ministers, seated in their accustomed places, calmly awaited them. They had decided to surrender without violence to prevent bloodshed, and the Red Guards led them away to the Fortress of St. Peter and St. Paul. Kerensky had already left to seek military aid, but he could not rally enough loyal troops to put up any appreciable resistance.

On the following day Lenin and Trotsky announced their

An Uzbek peasant receives a grant of land

triumph to the Second Congress of the Soviets of All Russia which was meeting in Petrograd. This was the exact timing that Lenin had planned. He had calculated that the Congress was likely to accept a victory that had already been won, and his gamble succeeded. By intrigue and bravado he had vanquished his political opponents; now he had to ignite "the world-wide socialist revolution."

In the first hours of Bolshevik rule Lenin made "the decree on land," proclaiming that every peasant had the right to own the land he worked on. It was an act diametrically opposed to the Marxist ideal of common ownership and to later Bolshevik practice, and it created a state of affairs which Lenin well knew could never last in a communist society. However, at this critical time he was dependent on the support of the peasants, and he dispatched messengers to every village to broadcast the decree.

Lenin and Trotsky adopted the crossed hammer and sickle as an emblem of industry and agriculture working together for the common good under proletarian rule. All over Russia the revolutionaries hoisted the Bolshevik banner where the imperial eagle had flown for centuries. The leaders agreed that the new executives in the Russian government should no longer be called ministers as in czarist times. They addressed each other as "comrade" but looked for an official title. Finally they settled on "commissar" as a fitting description of rank. Lenin became Chairman of the Council of the People's Commissars. He appointed Trotsky Commissar for Foreign Affairs; and Joseph Stalin, who had proved himself an able and ardent Bolshevik, Commissar for Nationalities, to deal with the many different national groups within the vast territories of Russia.

With the advent of Bolshevik power, government by open discussion ended in Russia. The Constituent Assembly was a dream of the past. The Congress of Soviets dispersed, and the delegates went home to proclaim proletarian rule. The commissars in Petrograd had little government experience and Lenin made all the decisions. The power of the Party and the reign of the secret police were to develop later. At this early stage most Bolsheviks probably would not have stood for mass murder and terrorist rule. They had objected to violence and were relieved that there had been so little bloodshed.

But Lenin faced almost insuperable administrative problems, for he inherited the chaos that he had helped to create, and the continuing stress of war. He had sworn to give the Russian people bread and peace. Now he had to fulfill these promises. He had persuaded the workers to strike and the troops to rebel. He had encouraged a cult of disobedience, disrupted industry, and swept away respect for law and order. Lenin saw clearly that if the Bolshevik regime was going to survive, he would have to introduce a new form of discipline, improve production, and come to terms with Germany.

8 · The Dictatorship of the Proletariat

AFTER HIS RETURN FROM EXILE Lenin adopted the name communist, rather than socialist, to describe his political party. By this means he separated the Bolsheviks from all the other Russian socialist parties and gave them an identity of their own.

On November 9, 1917, two days after the surrender of the Provisional Government, Trotsky broadcast an appeal to all the warring nations to agree to an armistice. The French and British —and also the Americans, who had declared war on Germany in April of that year—immediately protested. Above all they wanted Russia's armies to continue the war. But the Germans accepted the armistice proposal and, on December 5, signed a ten-day truce with Russia. A party of Bolshevik delegates, headed by Trotsky, set out from Petrograd for the distant Polish town of Brest-Litovsk to negotiate a peace treaty with a high-powered German diplomatic and military mission.

The Russian people were war-weary and longing for peace. But when the Germans published their conditions for ending hostilities, they were so harsh that an indignant outcry arose from every political faction and section of society. Trotsky had

Leon Trotsky, Commisar for War

sworn that he would "sign only an honorable peace," but now the Germans demanded that the defeated Russians grant independence to Poland; the Baltic states of Estonia, Lithuania and Latvia; and Finland. In addition, the Germans proposed to take over part of the Ukraine with its rich cornfields—the main granary of Russia. By the Treaty of Brest-Litovsk the Russians stood to lose a third of their population, their best farmland, their most important sources of oil, coal and iron, and almost all their Baltic ports. It was a crippling prospect, but it was in keeping with Lenin's declared policy of giving the people of different nationalities, many of whom had been forced into the Russian Empire by czarist conquest, a wider measure of independence.

When the Central Committee heard the terms of the treaty the leading Bolsheviks were fiercely divided. Lenin wanted to sign immediately, and Stalin, who was by this time beginning to make a name for himself in the party, supported him. All through the war Lenin had openly favored peace at any price except that of handing over Bolshevik political power to any other party. By December 1917 he was convinced that the morale of the German Army had been destroyed by communist propaganda and that Germany was on the verge of revolution. At the same time he had a realistic idea of the fighting strength of the Russian armies. He knew that their resistance was virtually at an end, and that there was little left for the Bolsheviks to bargain with.

Secret documents have since revealed the fact that the German Government was, at this time, paying millions of marks into the Bolsheviks' treasury, confident that of all the Russian political parties, the Bolsheviks were the most likely to destroy the Russian fighting spirit and make peace.

Nevertheless, Trotsky and many other prominent commissars stubbornly refused to accept the German demands. With Lenin's reluctant consent they entered into long, drawn-out peace negotiations but, toward the end of February 1918, German patience finally gave out, and the government issued an ultimatum giving the Russians forty-eight hours to come to terms. At the same time a German army received orders to march on Petrograd. The Bolsheviks, unable to repel the advancing armies, transferred the seat of government to Moscow and set up quarters in the Kremlin, the ancient palace of the czars. They also moved the ex-Czar Nicholas and his family from confinement in a Petrograd palace, eastward to the city of Ekaterinburg in the Ural Mountains, so that they would not fall into German hands.

The Central Committee of the Bolshevik Party met in a stormy session to debate the German ultimatum. For the first time since he had become head of the Party, Lenin threatened to resign if the commissars refused to accept the peace terms. Despondency and fear gripped the meeting, for there was no other man in Russia who had equal standing or was capable of wielding the same authority. Finally, to avoid an open split, Trotsky switched his support to Lenin. This was the vital vote, for it gave Lenin a majority of one in favor of making peace. Despite the concession he had made to save the Party, Trotsky could not bring himself to return to Brest-Litovsk. On March 3, a substitute delegation signed the treaty which most Russians considered an absolute disaster and the shameful surrender of a great nation.

Meanwhile, Lenin was extending communist control over domestic affairs. Despite the German contributions, the government was very short of money, and in December Lenin nationalized the twenty-eight main Russian banks by the simple method of sending twenty-eight detachments of sharpshooters to the head offices and arresting the directors. If they agreed to work for the government he allowed them to keep their jobs. If they refused, he sent them to prison and appointed Bolsheviks in their stead. He proceeded with the nationalization of industry more cautiously. It was almost impossible in the early days of the proletarian revolution to find men with adequate experience and skill to replace bourgeois managers and technicians. Many factories ground to a halt, many mills lay idle, and production was abysmally low.

In January 1918 Lenin addressed a political meeting in Petrograd, quoting words of advice that he had given to workers who had come to ask him how they should best use the property they had seized: ". . . you are the government, do as you please, take all you want, we will support you; but take care of production, see that production is useful. Take up useful work; you will make mistakes, but you will learn."

Lenin had the utmost respect for scientific achievement, and he looked forward to the day when Russia would take a leading place among the great industrial nations in a workers' world. But in 1918 he was hard pressed. He could not find the money, the men, the raw materials or the skill to manufacture even the ordinary necessities of life, or keep the power stations and trains in running order.

Lenin had always thought that bloodshed and mass terror must inevitably precede social change, and he had frequently quoted Karl Marx to his followers, telling them that no revolution in history had been accomplished without violence and desolation.

For years Russians had lived in dread of the *Okrana,* the

Felix Dzershinsky, Chief of the Cheka

czarist secret police. There had been general relief and rejoicing when the force was disbanded after the March Revolution. But the freedom from fear was short-lived, for Lenin swiftly invented an instrument of Party discipline even more comprehensive and crushing than that of the czars.

In December 1917, the same month that he took over the banks, Lenin summoned Felix Dzerzhinsky, a prominent Bolshevik noted for his fanatical attachment to the Party, and instructed him to form an Extraordinary Commission to Combat Revolution and Sabotage. The initials of this organization spelled *Cheka,* a name which soon brought alarm and despair to thousands of Russian homes.

Lenin chose the man for this key job with insight. Felix Dzerzhinsky was a well-tested revolutionary with a complex character, a mixture of idealism and savagery not unlike that of his master. He came from a respectable family of Polish gentry, and early in life developed a passionate desire to dedicate himself either to God or man. For a time he could not decide whether to become a Roman Catholic priest or a revolutionary. Having chosen the more daring career, Dzerzhinsky spent most of his adult years in prison or in exile in Siberia. He never wavered in his admiration for Lenin, and carried out his appointed task as director of the Cheka with unfailing thoroughness and devotion to duty.

Gradually many Bolsheviks who had protested against the use of armed force accepted mass terrorism as the only possible means of retaining political power. But there were still many people who had joined the Bolshevik Party who were shocked and revolted by Cheka methods, and openly decried them. One by one these dissenters fell victim to political purges and were executed or mysteriously disappeared. Lenin termed every critic of the regime "an enemy of the revolution," and in the first year of Bolshevik rule thousands were shot by Cheka gunmen without any semblance of trial or opportunity for defense.

After the signing of the Brest-Litovsk Treaty there was growing unrest throughout Russia, partly owing to the feeling by many Russians that they had been betrayed into making an unjust peace, and partly owing to the intervention of former allies. When Russia was still at war, the French, British and Americans had sent military aid in the form of arms and equipment to Vladivostok and other Far Eastern ports. In July 1918 they landed troops in Siberia to prevent these supplies from falling into German hands, hoping also to restart the war against Germany. At the same time, a legion of Czech soldiers who had fought as volunteers with the Russian armies took up arms against the Bolsheviks. They were joined by socialist revolutionaries, remnants of Cossack regiments and other opponents of the existing regime. Soon a vast area stretching from the Pacific coast to the Volga River was in the hands of this People's Army. Farther west, in the region of the Don River, General Kornilov—who had never given up hope of destroying the Bolshevik revolutionaries—joined other czarist generals to form what they called the White Army, as opposed to the Red. Together these generals collected scattered soldiers of their old regiments and marched against the Bolshevik forces.

On July 17, 1918, soon after the allied landings in Siberia, Czar Nicholas Romanov, his wife and children, his doctor and his personal staff were shot to death in the cellar of their lodgings in Ekaterinburg by Bolshevik command. The executioners hacked the bodies to pieces and burned them so that no trace remained. The following night remaining members of the royal family, imprisoned in a nearby town, were thrown down a mine shaft and left to die.

The true motive of these crimes has never been disclosed. It is possible that Lenin feared that the anti-communist forces would use the ex-Czar as a figurehead and a symbol of resistance. Another explanation historians put forward is that Comrade Lenin felt he must demonstrate to the world the inflexible purpose of communism; that he determined, by an act of exceptional brutality, to prove that nothing would be allowed to stand in the way of proletarian dictatorship, and that there could be no going back to any other form of government.

In the following month Lenin was shot at point-blank range by a woman, as a protest against Bolshevik suppression of the Constituent Assembly. He recovered from his wounds, but soon afterward his health began to deteriorate.

When Lenin's land decree first reached the villages the peasants had risen in a body to attack the landlords, sack their homes and seize the land. Thousands of aristocratic and well-to-do families were murdered in an uncontrollable storm of fury, and thousands more fled the country. In the cities the food situation grew steadily worse. Because most of the countryside had been laid waste, the peasants harvested scarcely enough grain for their own use and they doggedly refused to send any away. In a desperate effort to keep the few remaining factory workers at their jobs, Lenin ordered squads of men, often accompanied by units of the Cheka, to go out to the villages and requisition food. Some peasants had obtained land under the czars and owned large enough farms to pay for hired labor. They were known as *kulaks,* and as they were comparatively prosperous they became the main prey of the food gangs. If the kulaks had no stocks to hand over, or if they tried to hide their produce, the requisitioning parties shot them on the spot. Their grief-stricken families were filled with bitterness and hatred. They destroyed their cows and pigs and burned their crops rather than have them fall into the hands of government agents. The poorer peasants followed suit, and many left home and joined the People's Army to fight for their promised rights. The toll of civil war rose, and hunger and misery spread through Russia. It is estimated that in 1918 and 1919 nine million people died of disease, famine and cold.

Lenin appointed Trotsky Commissar for War as a reward for his loyalty at the time of Brest-Litovsk. This was a job which gave Trotsky an opportunity to exercise his many talents. Under his skillful and dynamic direction the Red Army became a powerful and disciplined force. At moments of danger he was in his element, appearing unexpectedly in his famous armored train, at the most exposed salients, and inspiring the men with his own enthusiasm and faith in victory.

An outstanding example of Lenin's greatness was his apparent detachment from the conduct of the Civil War. Though he watched every move on every front, he seldom interfered. Few dictators have managed to resist the temptation of leading their armies to victory, but Lenin was not interested in publicity. He had confidence in the future and he had the good sense to keep away from the battle fronts because he knew that Trotsky would handle the troops better than he. Lenin recognized Trotsky's weaknesses, his vanity and irrepressible love of dash and display. But he also appreciated the drive and the genius of his War Commissar and knew that he was doing an invaluable job. In return Trotsky did not question Lenin's dictatorship in matters of Party policy.

In the autumn of 1920 the Red Army defeated the White Army in southern Russia and captured the Crimea. Though there were occasional outbreaks of fighting during the next few years, the main battles of the Civil War were over. The Czech soldiers made their way home; the People's Army and the White

Army gradually dispersed. They had suffered from the lack of any real incentive. All the leaders could offer in return for victory was a revival of the old regime, and this had little appeal for the average Russian.

But, despite the success of the Red Army, the situation in Russia was deteriorating seriously and discontent was mounting. To win favor with the peasants who made up 80 per cent of the entire population, Russian Marxists had been forced to hand out land and encourage dreams of private ownership totally contradictory to Marx's principles and wholly impractical in a communist state.

For more than a hundred years people had striven not only for land and better living, but also for free elections and liberty of thought. After the proletarian revolution they expected to establish a chain of worker's councils, or soviets, each one composed of local representatives who would have the interests of the community at heart. They suddenly woke up to the hard fact that they had simply exchanged one form of tyranny for another, and that the seat of Bolshevik dictatorship was as remote as the courts of the czars. Often the only personal link with the government was the presence of the detested Cheka.

Moreover, the Russian people had never contemplated life without religion, but as soon as Lenin came to power he ordered the suppression of the Russian Orthodox Church. True to Marxist teaching, Lenin was a declared atheist. Long before the revolution he had written: "Religion is the opiate of the people, a sort of spiritual liquor, meant to make the slaves of capitalism drown their humanity and their desire for a decent existence." Within a few months churches, monasteries and convents were closed and religious colleges banned. Although schools were opened all over the country to end illiteracy, Christian teaching was forbidden in them. People continued to practice their religion in secret, but they missed the traditional ritual, warmth and beauty of the Orthodox services, and they resented communist interference.

When, faced by stubborn peasant resistance, the requisitioning squads failed to produce food for the townspeople, Lenin declared all private enterprise and all trading outside government centers illegal. He sent out commissars to shut down every shop

A class to end illiteracy

and market so that farmers were compelled to sell their goods at any price the government decided to pay. The farmers received the new restrictions with wrathful indignation.

In March 1921 the sailors at the naval base on the island fortress of Kronstadt, close to Petrograd, rose in revolt. These men had been the backbone of the revolution, and they had fought fiercely to put Lenin in power. Now they demanded free elections and an end to repression. Lenin and Trotsky sent picked Red Army units to put down the rising, but the troops refused to fire on the rebel sailors. Cheka gunmen, attached to the Red Army to prevent desertions, carried out their orders and shot every fifth soldier. Trotsky sent in fresh forces to storm the fortress, but the sailors refused to surrender. They defended the island until thousands lay dead in the streets and the attacking force had suffered equal losses. On March 17 the mutiny was finally quelled and the Kronstadt guns were silenced. The surviving sailors were shot by Cheka guards or sentenced to hard labor in Siberia.

After the Kronstadt revolt Lenin realized that if the Bolsheviks were going to survive, he would have to make some compromise to pacify the people. He therefore introduced a new economic policy, the NEP, which permitted some private trade and set up a wage system by which people were paid according to the value of their labor, rather than according to their needs, as in a socialist state. At this time of crisis Lenin admitted that it had been a mistake to try to introduce true communism at such an early stage in proletarian rule.

But in general, during the years of hardship and at the

climax of disillusionment, Lenin had remained comparatively calm and confident. Marx had always predicted that revolution would be a stormy process and Lenin had never counted on an easy victory. He still had faith in world socialism, and he regarded the collapse of Germany and the abdication of Emperor William II in 1918 as a step in a revolutionary direction. He was not worried when the capitalist governments treated the Bolsheviks as outlaws and murderers. He was so certain that these same capitalists were doomed to extinction that it did not matter to him what they thought or how they behaved.

Although Lenin was wrong in his forecast of international events, he was correct in summing up the weakness of anticommunist resistance within Russia. He calculated that the bourgeois opposition was confused and divided, and he was convinced that in the long run it would not stand up to the terrorist activities of the Cheka and the mighty propaganda program which he had drawn up for the Communist Party.

In 1919 Lenin had overhauled the Party organization. To avoid what he considered fruitless, time-wasting debate, he set up, within the Central Committee, the Politburo—a small group of trusted men on whom he could rely to ratify without delay the decisions he had already made. The original members of the Politburo were Lenin, Trotsky, Kamenev, Bukharin, and Stalin. They had fought for the revolution, but their triumph was soon over. When Stalin came to power, all these men—the Old Guard of Bolshevism—were tried for treason and executed. The only exception was Trotsky, who was deported from the Soviet Union and later murdered by a communist agent.

In the same year that Lenin instituted the Politburo, he

also founded the Comintern, using a name coined from the words Communist International. This was an organization designed to carry out a historic task and set world revolution alight. The Twenty One Points of the Comintern were a directive for communist action outside Russia, and remain so today. They were compiled by Lenin and although the Comintern ceased to exist during the Second World War, Soviet communist policy has changed little and, in fifty years, no one has produced a better blueprint for disrupting industry and creating chaos in order to weaken capitalist society. Lenin directed every organization that wished to work with the Comintern to remove from its list any members with leanings toward trade unionism, or with any respect for conventional reform, and replace them with reliable communists dedicated to the cause of revolution. At the same time, the points of the Comintern instructed communist parties in countries outside the Soviet Union to form revolutionary cells within the trade unions and every other working-class organization in order to undermine the existing leadership and capture overall control.

Lenin was a man of simple tastes. He was not vain and he did not seek personal glory. He despised hero-worship and resisted every move his followers made to place him on a pedestal. He accepted power as a matter of course and became a supreme dictator because he saw no other way of consolidating the revolution. He was absolutely ruthless in the cause of communism, and he had no mercy for anyone who allowed personal feelings to conflict with the aims of the Communist Party. Though he acquired money for Party funds by questionable means, there is no evidence to show that he ever took for himself a single ruble more than he needed for frugal day-to-day living. He occupied an apartment in the Kremlin with his wife Krupskaya, his sister Maria and one maid. When there was not enough to eat in Moscow he was embarrassed by gifts of food parcels and passed them on to others he felt were more deserving.

Lenin loved the mountains and forests and he spent all his holidays in the countryside trying to cast off the heavy cares of office and build new strength. With Krupskaya, he walked or bicycled, went fishing or swimming, and stayed in mountain huts or country inns where the people were friendly and treated him as an equal. Although he had no children of his own he loved young people. Trotsky's young sons greeted Lenin with shouts of delight and he was gay and relaxed in their company.

During the last years of his life Lenin suffered increasing ill health. He had acute headaches and great difficulty in sleeping, followed by fits of dizziness and overpowering exhaustion; but the doctors could not diagnose the cause. He grew increasingly irritable, intolerant of detail and impatient with inefficiency. In May 1922 he had his first stroke, which left him paralyzed on the right side and affected his speech. With indomitable will power Lenin struggled to regain his lost faculties. His mind was clear, but he had to learn to talk again, and with infinite patience Krupskaya taught him to write with his left hand. By October he was back at work, but he never again had the strength to exert his earlier authority.

During Lenin's illness a bitter battle for power developed in the Politburo. Trotsky, still Commissar for War, and Stalin, who had recently been appointed to the powerful post of Secretary General of the Politburo, were foremost among Lenin's would-be successors. Outwardly they planned for his return, but behind the scenes they jockeyed for the leading position.

In mid-December 1922, while in the little village of Gorki, thirty miles from Moscow, Lenin had a second stroke. It left him seriously incapacitated and he must have felt that the end was near. After a week he recovered sufficiently to dictate. He made no will, but left instead a memorandum, or testament, setting down his fears of a split in the Bolshevik Party after his death. On January 4 he added a postscript in which he tried to choose a man, or men, to succeed him. It is evident that he found it very difficult. He accused Stalin of lack of caution in using the enormous power he had gained, and criticized Trotsky for over-confidence. He complained that Bukharin, a younger member of the Central Committee, was not fully Marxist and had never really understood the dialectic, and that Piatakov, another young member, was wanting in political judgment. Lenin ended by recommending the removal of Stalin from the post of General Secretary, but he made no suggestion for his replacement.

On January 21, 1924, at the age of fifty-four, Lenin had a third, and fatal, stroke.

Within a few hours Stalin and other members of the Politburo arrived at Gorki. Two days later they took Lenin's body to the House of Trade Unions in Moscow. There it lay in state for four days while leading Bolsheviks kept guard and hundreds of thousands of mourners filed past to pay their last homage to the founder of communism.

Lenin lies in state, 1924

Despite the misery and disappointment of the last few years the Russian people remembered Lenin as a defender of their rights, a champion of the revolution, the man who gave them the promise of a society where men were free and equal.

On the day of the funeral the coffin was borne by members of the Politburo in a solemn procession through snowy streets lined with silent crowds. From dawn to dusk representatives of foreign communist parties and delegates from all over Russia laid their wreaths by Lenin's bier. At the end of the day it was surrounded by a mountain of flowers.

The body of Vladimir Ulyanov was embalmed and placed in the crypt of a majestic mausoleum by the walls of the Kremlin. Here it soon became a sacred shrine and place of pilgrimage for millions of peasants whose religious rites had been abolished since the revolution, and who felt the need of a shrine as a center of worship. Krupskaya protested, and there is no doubt that Lenin, with his horror of pomp and ceremony, would have greatly preferred to be laid to rest in a quiet grave deep in the countryside. But the Communist Party honored Lenin as a saint, and his body remains today exposed to public view, a figure of awe and veneration.

Lenin never turned aside from the role that he believed himself destined to play. He felt he was caught up in the wheels of history, a humble servant of events beyond human control. Although he was forced to adapt some Marxist theories to current Russian demands, he founded a great socialist state and he never doubted the eventual triumph of violent social change throughout the world.

9 · *Man of Steel*

JOSEPH DJUGASHVILI, successor to Lenin and an absolute dictator for almost thirty years, was born in 1879 at Gori, a little town in Georgia in southern Russia. His parents had both been serfs, liberated shortly before their marriage. They were free, but desperately poor. His father was a shoemaker and his mother worked as a washerwoman to help pay for the two-room hovel where the family lived. The first three Djugashvili babies died in quick succession, but Joseph turned out to be a strong child. His mother was a woman of great character, deeply religious and, despite her poverty, highly ambitious for her son. She lived long enough to share in his success, and when she visited him in the Kremlin people remarked on her quiet dignity.

She sent him at the age of nine to the Greek Orthodox Church school in Gori. Five years later she accepted for him, with immense pride and relief, a scholarship for the Theological Seminary at Tiflis, the capital of the Caucasus. She had always prayed that Joseph would become a priest, and it seemed that her prayers would be answered.

Joseph was clever and industrious, and he did well at his work. Every year he was at, or near, the top of his class. But very early in life he assessed the unfair advantages of inherited wealth; he recognized class differences and resented them. At the seminary he was conscious of his humble background and saw that the sons of the gentry despised his shabby clothes and peasant manners.

The region of Georgia contained a number of ancient tribal kingdoms, recently annexed by the Russian Empire. The people were tough and rebellious, proud of their national traditions and intolerant of Russian rule. Walled in by the towering snow-capped Caucasus Mountains in the north, and protected by the Black Sea on the west, they were shut off from the rest of Russia. They spoke their own language and preserved their ancient customs. So Joseph grew up in a country fiercely anti-czarist, seething with tribal feuds and revolutionary intrigue.

He was an avid reader, interested in folklore, history and politics, and always ready to take part in a heated debate. While he was still at the seminary he joined a patriotic group, working for Georgian freedom. But he soon became converted to Marxist doctrines and turned his energies from fighting for a narrow nationalism to promoting world-wide socialism. In his final year at the seminary the monks expelled him because they felt he was becoming a disturbing influence.

Joseph then threw himself into a full-time revolutionary life. With other young socialists, he awaited impatiently the clandestine deliveries of *Iskra,* pored over Lenin's writings, and called himself "an *Iskra* man." When he was twenty-two years old he was elected a member of the Social Democratic Committee of Tiflis and was sent to Batum, a new oil town near the

Turkish frontier, to organize socialist action and stir up labor trouble. Batum had a mixed population of Georgians, Armenians and Turks. It was rife with national discord, restless with expanding industry, and was a fertile field for socialist propaganda. Like most other conspirators, Joseph Djugashvili assumed a false name to escape identification by the police. He chose to be known as Koba, the Turkish word for indomitable. In Batum he set up a secret printing press to publish his own revolutionary leaflets. In 1902 he was arrested and imprisoned in the Batum jail. Here he set himself a rigid regime of study until, in the following year, he was deported to Siberia, far from the sources of Marxist literature.

The war with Japan was approaching and the tide of revolution was rising. Koba wasted no time in banishment. Early in 1904 he escaped, made his way over the frozen Siberian wastes in a peasant's cart, and arrived safely back in Tiflis.

The following year Koba met Lenin for the first time. Later he recorded his disappointment at this initial meeting. He had expected to pay homage to an outstanding and stately figure, and found instead an undistinguished-looking little man with simple manners and no obvious air of greatness. But he soon fell under Lenin's spell, and learned to respect his intellectual eminence, his organizing power and his mastery of men. When the Mensheviks and Bolsheviks separated, Koba immediately joined the Bolshevik faction. On his return to Tiflis he translated many of Lenin's writings into Georgian.

Koba played no part in the 1905 revolution which followed the massacre of Bloody Sunday. When the widespread strikes and uprisings died down, Lenin was in exile abroad and the Bolsheviks had little support at home. During the next few years Koba helped to organize bank raids to seize money for Party funds. He acted as a liaison between the Central Committee of the Bolshevik Party and the armed squads who carried out the holdups. There were more raids in his area of the Caucasus than in any other part of Russia, and the most daring and profitable of all took place in Tiflis.

Gradually Koba gained valuable experience in Party organization. He did not, at this stage, seek promotion, but worked behind the scenes, building a reputation for his dogged perseverance and strong nerves. Though he spent seven of the ten years between 1907 and 1917 in prison, his services were rewarded and he was elected in 1912 to the Central Committee of the Bolshevik Party. Lenin needed men who were both loyal and efficient, and he undoubtedly checked on Koba's record and found it satisfactory. From this time onward Joseph Djugashvili took the name of Stalin—Man of Steel.

In March 1917, after the political amnesty, the exiles flocked back to Petrograd. Trotsky and Stalin came with them. Both were thirty-eight years old and had worked for the revolutionary cause since boyhood. Trotsky became head of the Petrograd Soviet and made a name for himself as an orator and a guiding spirit in the new regime. Stalin became editor of *Pravda,* the official Bolshevik newspaper, but he was content to remain in the background, feeling his way toward fame and methodically gathering up the reins of future power. The general public had never heard of him.

The Czarist secret police record of Joseph Stalin

After the October Revolution Stalin received his first major post when Lenin appointed him Commissar for Nationalities, to deal with the many different non-Russian peoples who had been conquered by the czars and attached to the empire. They varied enormously in language, appearance, culture and social development—from the Yakuts tending their herds of reindeer on the edge of the Arctic Circle, to the Asian Kazakhs near the Chinese frontier, the sturdy Ukrainians who had lived for hundreds of years on the rich farmland of the Ukraine, and the rugged Georgians in Stalin's homeland who are reputed to live longer than any other known people. Despite their outward differences these conquered people had something in common, for they all resented Russian annexation and demanded individual rights and some degree of self-government.

On November 2, 1922, from his Kremlin commissariat, Stalin made a Declaration of the Rights of the Peoples of Russia, which he and Lenin had drawn up together. The Declaration granted non-Russian minorities equality, sovereignty and self-determination, rights which Stalin did not recognize when he came to power.

At this time the Bolsheviks renamed their country. The Empire became the Union of Soviet Socialist Republics (USSR), and soon after Lenin's death the city of Petrograd was renamed Leningrad in his honor, but the seat of government remained in Moscow.

Almost imperceptibly Stalin tightened his hold on the Communist Party machine. He became Commissar of the Workers' and Peasants' Inspectorate, an organization set up to supervise and purify the whole system of government, and also a member of the Politburo. On April 3, 1922, he was appointed Secretary General of the Central Committee of the Communist Party. By this time Lenin was ill and the struggle for the succession was well under way.

Stalin had always recognized Trotsky as his most dangerous rival. Head of the Red Army and victor of the civil war, Trotsky had become a Bolshevik hero with immense popular appeal. Unlike Stalin, he was a polished politician. He had built up a public image and he spoke fluently and wrote well. He had traveled in western European countries and collected firsthand knowledge of foreign conditions and customs.

But when Lenin died in January 1924, Stalin had maneuvered himself into an almost impregnable position in the Party without ever appearing to grind down his opponents. It was a feat of political genius. He played his cards so carefully and remained so inconspicuous that most of his colleagues underestimated his strength. Outwardly he appeared moderate and cooperative. Actually he was waiting for his rivals to make mistakes and was systematically edging them out of the race. He formed a close alliance with Kamenev and Zinoviev, members of the Politburo and Bolsheviks of long-standing, and encouraged them to block Trotsky's path to power for their own good.

In the autumn of 1924 Stalin veered sharply away from the Marx-Lenin doctrine of world revolution and the dictatorship of an international proletariat. He was not an idealist and he knew that a "classless world" was a distant dream. He also saw that the prospect of "perpetual revolution" would have no practical appeal to a people weary of hardship, shortages and strife. For the first time he coined the slogan "socialism in one country" and encouraged national pride. He recalled the exploits of Russian heroes like Alexander Nevski who, in the thirteenth century, had repulsed all foreign invaders and had been canonized a saint of the Russian Orthodox Church for his valor and victory. Stalin spoke of "Mother Russia" as the sole center of a new civilization and urged Russian communists to press on to prosperity without waiting for the capitalist countries to set up revolutionary governments. But in the aftermath of revolution and civil war there was widespread poverty and disillusionment in Russia. The only way that Stalin could improve his own position was by putting the blame for the country's plight on his political opponents. In 1925 he accused Trotsky of betraying the Party and

Sowing by hand as in Czarist Russia

engineered his resignation as Commissar for War. Once Trotsky was defeated, Stalin no longer needed the support of Kamenev and Zinoviev, so he began to undermine their authority. It suddenly became clear to the Politburo that Stalin reigned supreme, and the Communist Party had become a weapon of one man's will.

In 1928 Stalin decided to revolutionize the entire economy. He planned, by a series of Five Year Plans, to transform the USSR from an impoverished agricultural country to a powerful industrial state, no matter what it cost the long-suffering peasantry. Party agents first attacked the peasants who had refused to send the towns produce which they needed for their own families. To begin with, only the poorest peasants were forced to put their small holdings into large collective farms, where they were promised a regular wage and better living. But the Five Year Plan soon spread to every farmer in the land, and wholesale collectivization was accomplished with bloodshed and widespread misery. Farmers who clung to their property were driven out with machine guns, but they slaughtered their livestock and set fire to their grain rather than hand it over to the state, precisely as they had done in Lenin's day. The kulaks, or well-to-do peasants, had more to lose than the others, and resisted most

Harvesting on a collective farm

fiercely of all. Stalin saw that they were likely to cause trouble in the collective farms, so he determined to wipe them out altogether and seize their well-ordered homesteads. In a highly organized and completely merciless military operation, two million kulaks and their families were either deported to empty lands in Siberia, where they had no means of making a living, or used as forced labor in the coal mines of the Donets Valley or the salt mines in the far north, under such terrible conditions that there was little chance of survival.

In 1932 Stalin's young wife Nadia Alliluyeva, who had been absolutely devoted to him, committed suicide. Stalin's political policy had caused a rift in their marriage and it is believed that she could not bear to have any part in the tragic consequences of his pitiless oppression.

As part of the first Five Year Plan whole villages were evacuated and the inhabitants drafted into factories, or put to work on bridges and dams, oil refineries and power stations, roads and railways. No one provided new homes to go with the new jobs and countless thousands of peasants died of exposure, hunger, thirst and disease. This was the first of a succession of Five Year Plans. The cost in human life, mass suffering and loss of individual freedom can never be calculated. However, the Russian peasants were accustomed to toil and hardship; miraculously they reached and even surpassed the tremendous industrial targets they were set. In 1930 the great Zaporozhye Dam was completed across the Dnieper River to provide electric power for Ukrainian industry. In ten years the USSR was beginning to compete with the most advanced nations of the West.

But it appears that agriculture was sacrificed to industry and in the long run the collective farms have not come up to expectations. The peasants did not work as hard for the state as they did on their own land, and, in spite of government concessions and added incentives, there have been a number of years when they did not produce enough food to support the growing population.

Education was given high priority in the programs of the successive Five Year Plans. In czarist Russia most peasants were completely illiterate; but Marx stressed the importance of a people educated in socialist ideology, and both Lenin and Stalin saw the need of a nation equipped to compete with the capitalist world in science and culture. Thousands of new schools were built and millions of children were taught to read and write. At the same time they learned the importance of absolute obedience and unswerving loyalty to the Party, according to the communist principle of weakening family ties in order to strengthen the solidarity of the community as a whole.

The Party took over control of every aspect of life. The radio, the theater, the films, the press and every other form of communication became channels for Party propaganda. People were directed where they should work, how they should spend their leisure and what they should read. Above all they were discouraged from thinking for themselves because the Party had already made the necessary decisions.

Lenin had changed the official title of the Party from Bolshevik to Communist. But even in Stalin's day, by Marxist standards, the Soviet Union was a socialist state working toward communism. Stalin respected the essential Marxist principle which forbade a business concern or a private individual to employ labor for personal profit. But, like Lenin in the NEP, he made concessions to forestall rebellion, keep the Party in power, and step up production. In order to carry out the Five Year Plans, Stalin needed new factories and up-to-date machinery, and he was desperately short of experienced men to build and run them. He re-called the bourgeois managers and technicians who had lost their jobs after the revolution and gave them teaching posts in newly founded technical and industrial schools. When young communists acquired these necessary skills they were worth their weight in rubles and Stalin paid them accordingly, and gave them special privileges and better housing than the rest. He also offered tempting awards to workers who exceeded the normal rate of production. As a result, coal miners and workers in steel mills and factories chalked up remarkable results and were duly presented with medals and bonuses and were honored as supermen of the Soviet Union. Stalin regarded this preferential treatment as a temporary measure, and looked forward to the day when pure communism would prevail and every citizen would be paid "according to his needs."

Marx had visualized social change rising from the bottom up, generated by the inequalities of life and carried out by the will of the people. Stalin could not wait for the natural process. He imposed drastic change by means of totalitarian power.

In the course of the Five Year Plans, Stalin's policy underwent a violent change. In 1929 the Party line denounced all Social Democratic parties as enemies of the working class, un-

A labor lesson in a Moscow school

worthy of communist support. But in 1935, after the rise of Adolf Hitler in Germany, communists were encouraged to make friends and form alliances with Social Democrats and anyone else who could help them.

In 1934 Sergei Kirov, the able young governor of Leningrad, was murdered by a young assassin who did not disclose his motives before he was executed. It is generally assumed that Kirov was killed by Stalin's orders because he was becoming too popular. This crime opened the way to a grim succession of brutal purges. For five years the rest of the world looked on in horror while Stalin wiped out every shadow of opposition and reduced the government of the USSR to a body of yes-men who meekly obeyed his commands. Almost all the Bolshevik Old Guard, the men who had fought passionately for the revolution and finally carried the Party to victory, were executed or exiled. They were arrested by the secret police—then known as the OGPU and later as the NKVD—and tried on trumped-up charges of plotting against the Party, trying to assassinate Stalin, treating with capitalist countries, or inciting sabotage. The chiefs of the Red Army and a great many of the serving officers were accused of being in league with the Germans and were shot without trials. Members of the secret police suffered the same fate they had handed out to "the enemies of the people." Some of the victims had no hearing at all, but others appeared for a grotesque mock trial. In prison they had been subjected to physical torture and mental agony through threats of reprisals on their families. In the witness box, to protect their wives and children, many of the accused confessed to monstrous crimes which they had obviously never committed, and their admissions of guilt always ended with profuse praise of Stalin and all his works. His former associates, Kamenev and Zinoviev, were accused of planning Kirov's murder and executed with the rest. Official records of the purges do not exist, but it is certain that many thousands of innocent people were put to death without a vestige of evidence against them. It seemed that Stalin dared not leave a single man in office capable of leading, or brave enough to support, an opposition group. By 1939 the country was drained of politicians of conviction and courage and the purges drew to a somber close.

In 1928 Trotsky had been exiled to Turkistan in southern Russia as a punishment for his opposition to Stalin. The following year he was banished and began his wanderings, first to Constantinople, then to Norway. Finally he settled in Mexico. He had never ceased to protest in his writings against the evils of Stalin's misrule. During his exile a Moscow tribunal sentenced him to death for treachery. In the summer of 1940 a communist agent carried out the death sentence. As Trotsky sat at his desk engaged in writing a critical life of Stalin, the assassin shattered his skull with an ax. Europe was aflame with war and the crime passed almost unnoticed.

10 · Stalin and the Spread of Socialism

WHILE STALIN TIGHTENED HIS GRIP on the Soviet Union, political tension was mounting in Europe. In Italy, Benito Mussolini had overthrown a liberal government and carried the Fascist Party to supreme power. In Germany, Adolf Hitler rose from obscurity to become an absolute dictator, head of the National Socialist, or Nazi, Party and Chancellor of the German State. The Italian and German dictators were both fiercely anti-Bolshevist and Hitler was also fanatically anti-Jewish.

Stalin watched the rise of these hostile governments with bitter hatred and intense alarm. In speech after speech Hitler swore to exterminate the "Jewish Bolsheviks," and Stalin replied with abuse of the "Nazi scum." But he was very much afraid, for he knew that Hitler had built up a massive military machine and that in a month of war all the hard-won industrial gains in the USSR could be swept away.

Stalin determined to keep peace for the Soviet Union at any price. He had already made tentative advances to Germany but he had not succeeded in concluding a treaty. Therefore, he turned to France and Britain and tried to form a coalition against Hitler. In the spring of 1939 Stalin was negotiating with both sides. His approaches to the British and French governments met with a cool reception. Despite Stalin's declared policy of "socialism in one country," Bolsheviks were regarded as dangerous troublemakers. Enthusiastic communists in western Europe had created Popular Fronts and organized strikes and labor disputes. Even more important, people in the west had been deeply shocked by the murder of the Russian royal family and by Stalin's purges.

In 1936 civil war had broken out in Spain between a republican government and a nationalist army led by General Francisco Franco. Communists, many of them foreign volunteers, fought along with the Republicans, and Stalin backed them with arms and money. German Nazis and Italian Fascists supported General Franco and for nearly three years Spain was torn apart by a brutal and merciless war. In January 1939 Franco was victorious and the foreign forces went home. It was estimated that the civil war had cost a million lives, and it was evident that the Spanish people had suffered poverty and despair while three rival dictators tested their powers of destruction.

In the western world the Bolshevik regime was associated with bloodshed, and democratic leaders were reluctant to enter into a treaty with a government they condemned and distrusted. Also many of them thought that if Hitler was really bent on agression he would attack Stalin, his declared enemy, and leave western Europe alone. Having failed to come to terms with France and Britain, Stalin saw that the only alternative was to treat with the Nazis in the hope that this would encourage Hitler to attack the west.

The Soviet Union 1939

War records have since shown that Hitler had little to gain from victory in western Europe but prestige. His main ambitions were centered on conquest in the East. He wanted everything that Russia had to offer: *lebensraum,* or living space, for the overcrowded German people; food from the wheat fields of the Ukraine, and fuel from the rich oil fields of the Caucasus. Stalin had nothing to gain from any war and everything to lose. He could only hope that Hitler would be so exhausted by a war in the west that he would never be able to tackle Russia.

In August 1939 Stalin and Hitler announced the signing of a non-aggression pact by which they promised not to attack each other, under any circumstances whatsoever, for at least ten years. Later it became known that they had also secretly agreed to seize and share territories in eastern Europe. It was an infamous contract between two unscrupulous dictators, both seeking their own ends and both playing for time. Hitler calculated that the pact would keep Stalin quiet while he conquered the west, and Stalin gained a respite to strengthen his defenses against the German attack he trusted he would never have to meet.

The pact struck fear into the hearts of the peace-loving people of the world, and events gathered terrifying speed. Hitler had gained a very strong position before he made the pact with Stalin. In March 1938 he had taken over Austria, and in March 1939 he moved into Czechoslovakia. He accomplished these conquests by terrorism, trickery and false promises, and by winning local support in key spots throughout both countries. At the final stages he put up a show of force, but he never had to fire a single shot.

At the end of August 1939, flushed with his bloodless victories, and fortified by his pact with Stalin, Hitler attacked Poland. Britain and France observed a defense pact they had made with Poland and declared war on Germany. The Poles fought gallantly against hopeless odds, but Hitler swept in from the west and Stalin, in accordance with the terms of the pact, sent the Red Army into eastern Poland. In four weeks Polish resistance was crushed.

So far the war had gone according to Hitler's plan, and he turned to the west, hoping to make peace with Britain and split the Anglo-French alliance. When the peace move failed he mobilized his forces to conquer western Europe by armed force.

Stalin followed every movement of the war in the west with extreme anxiety. When Hitler made lightning conquests of Denmark, Norway, Holland, Belgium and France, Stalin's fears increased. He saw that every Nazi victory hastened the subjugation of Western Europe and freed Nazi armed forces for an attack on Russia.

By the spring of 1941, the Germans had not managed to defeat Britain, but there was no escape from Hitler's madness. He had set his heart on the invasion of Russia, and although he had to keep troops in the West, he decided to go ahead and fight on two fronts. He briefed his generals for "Operation Barbarossa," telling them that the Bolsheviks were an inferior and barbaric people, to be wiped off the face of the earth. The ordinary laws of war would not apply in Russia. He ordered every officer to carry out the campaign without regard for the civilian population. The troops must seize what they needed and live off the land. Hitler had witnessed the communist defeat in Spain and

Stalin during World War II

he had a poor opinion of the Red Army. He was certain that it was no match for his experienced and victorious forces and that the whole campaign would be over in two months.

On May 1, 1941, Stalin staged an impressive parade of military might in the Red Square in Moscow. A few days later he gave up the position of General Secretary of the Party and became Premier of the Soviet Union. In the same month Winston Churchill, Prime Minister of Great Britain, warned him that Hitler was massing his forces on the Russian frontier. It is curious that—although Stalin distrusted Hitler—he could not believe he would really strike.

At early dawn on June 21, 1941, the German air force roared over the frontier and armored divisions attacked in overwhelming force. The Red Army reeled back.

On July 3, in an Order of the Day, Stalin announced to his people a policy of "scorched earth." He commanded that: "In case of a forced retreat . . . all rolling stock must be evacuated, the enemy must not be left a single engine, a single railway car, a single pound of grain, or gallon of fuel. All valuable property . . . must be destroyed without fail. Sabotage groups must be formed to . . . blow up bridges and roads, damage telephone and telegraph lines, set fire to forests, stores and transport. In occupied regions conditions must be made unbearable for the enemy. They must be hounded and annihilated at every step. . . ." This was a direct appeal to patriotism, the people of one nation fighting for their country against a foreign enemy. Marx's and Lenin's doctrine of the international brotherhood of the working classes had given way under the stress of total war.

But Stalin had forged an iron discipline and it did not crack. He called for unbounded sacrifice and the people obeyed.

In the opening years of the war, the Red Army suffered fearful defeats. With swift encircling movements, German armored divisions surrounded the Russian forces and took more than a million prisoners. Following Hitler's commands, Nazi generals showed no mercy to the civilian population. They rounded up the political commissars and shot them, and they carried off every able-bodied man and woman for forced labor for the German war effort. Old people and children were left to die. The Russians were consumed with burning hatred and a longing for revenge.

But although the Red Army lost so many men, the High Command did not consider total surrender. German tanks reached a point only thirty miles from Moscow, and besieged Leningrad for ninety days while six hundred thousand people died of starvation. But gradually the Red Army learned to fight its way out of encirclement, and to use the vast spaces to absorb the attack and destroy the invaders. As the Nazis drove deeper and deeper into Russian territory, their lines of communication became perilously thin, and Hitler found—as Napoleon had found before him—that the Russian winter was a bitter enemy. He had prepared Operation Barbarossa for a brief summer campaign and his troops were not equipped for arctic blizzards.

Finally, at the end of 1942, the Red Army made a stand at the city of Stalingrad. The city was particularly important to Stalin because of his pride in its name, and its strategic position on the banks of the Volga, at the gateway to the Caucasus, guarding the rich oil fields of Baku. Stalin ordered the garrison "not to take one step back." With a strong counter-attack the Russians trapped the Sixth German Army of two hundred and fifty thousand men in the ruined city. On January 31, 1943, after seven weeks of agonizing siege, the ninety thousand survivors

The siege of Leningrad

surrendered. It was the turning point of the war. In a series of gigantic battles the Red Army drove the Nazi forces from the Caucasus to the center of Berlin. In the summer of 1944 American and British forces landed in France and fought their way eastward. By May 1945 the Germans were hemmed in on all sides and they signed an unconditional surrender.

In the following month, by joint declaration, the Soviet Union, the United States, Britain and France moved into Germany and Austria. Each nation controlled an occupation zone. Berlin, the former German capital, was divided into sectors, a four-power island within the Soviet zone of East Germany.

But as the danger receded, the wartime unity of the victorious nations wore thin and they could not agree on a postwar policy. The three Western powers planned to keep their occupation forces in the conquered countries only until the people had blotted out Nazism and relearned the system of democratic government. But the Russians had a different plan. They had suffered the greatest losses and damage from Nazi aggression and were determined that the Germans should never be in a position to attack again. They were resolved to occupy Eastern Germany indefinitely, and make it a communist bastion in Europe.

Stalin had held a magnificent victory parade in Moscow. Standing on top of the Lenin Mausoleum with Marshal Zhukov —the victor of many battles—by his side, he took the salutes of regiment after regiment as they swept by, flinging down captured German standards in a tattered heap before him. This was Stalin's hour of triumph. Memories of the cruelties of the prewar years were drowned in the exultation of victory. He was acclaimed the "Hero of the Soviet Union" and Generalissimo of the Red Army. But he must have looked ahead with grave misgivings, for in all Russia he was probably the only man who was fully aware of the terrible price the country had paid for the victory.

The official casualty lists recorded seven million dead, but the real figure was probably three times greater. Of the living,

Captured Nazi standards

millions were crippled, starving and ill. Cities and towns were devastated, farmland laid waste, factories and oil wells wrecked, transport almost nonexistent, and there were few remaining rubles in the communist treasury to repair the desolation.

Driven by sheer necessity and backed by an unrelenting sense of purpose, Stalin put the Russians back to work. Millions of them were homeless and in rags, but the Americans had exploded an atomic bomb, and Stalin used this scientific success as a challenge. He described the bomb as a threat to Soviet survival and, by a flood of anti-capitalist propaganda, spurred on Soviet workers to outpace American production, and Soviet scientists to rival American nuclear power.

Meanwhile a new international body had come into being. In June 1945 the United Nations Organization was founded with fifty member nations; and the United States, the Soviet Union, Britain, France and China became permanent members of the Security Council. The declared aims of the UN were to preserve peace and promote prosperity, but some member nations were not in a position to take advantage of United Nations help. Czechoslovakia, Poland, Hungary, Rumania and Bulgaria—the countries bordering the Soviet Union in the west—ended the war impoverished and in a political ferment. The Western powers hoped that with the help of UNRRA, the United Nations Relief and Rehabilitation Administration, and other United Nations agencies, these countries would be able to rebuild their ruined economies and, in the course of time, hold free elections and form stable governments.

But Stalin had other ideas. He saw the plight of these countries as an opportunity to extend communist influence and create a ring of satellite states which would protect Russia against the West. Moreover, he intended to squeeze food and raw materials from them to speed up Soviet recovery, without Western interference.

As the German armies had retreated, Soviet forces had moved in, followed by political agents and commissars. Gradually, in the capitals of Warsaw, Prague, Sofia, Bucharest and

Planting the hammer and sickle in Berlin

Budapest—with mock elections backed by armed force—Stalin installed the governments of his choice, headed by puppet leaders who took their orders from Moscow. He called these satellite states People's Democracies. They were not as advanced in socialist practice as the USSR, but they were detached from the capitalist system of the West.

In 1947 the American Secretary of State, General George Marshall, working with other government departments, produced a plan (which was to bear his name) aimed at helping the war-damaged nations to build new lives by planned financial aid. Stalin turned it down for the Soviet Union and compelled the

People's Democracies to refuse it also. In order to claim Marshall Plan Aid he would have had to produce a detailed inventory of Russian resources and needs. Far from revealing the state of Russian weakness to the world, he dared not tell even his own people the tragic truth lest they give way to utter despair.

Instead he encouraged them with tales of even greater suffering in the countries under capitalist rule, and he imposed a rigid censorship, the famous "Iron Curtain," shutting in the Soviet Union and the satellite states, so that their people could not compare their living conditions with those in the Western world. He behaved as though the Soviet Union had defeated Germany single-handed, and he was determined that communist loyalty should not be disturbed by the slightest glimmer of gratitude to the United States for its part in the war or its help in the peace.

Soon he encountered rebellion within the communist camp, and for the first time a fellow communist defied his authority. In Yugoslavia during the war, Marshal Tito—a revolutionary leader trained in Moscow—had commanded a gallant army of guerrillas against the far-stronger Nazi occupation forces. When the war ended Tito formed a communist government, but he resolved to run Yugoslavia on more nationalistic lines than the other East European countries which had become satellite states completely subservient to Moscow. He saw advantages in dealing with the West and refused to toe the Russian Communist Party line. Stalin furiously condemned Tito's action and excommunicated him from the Cominform—an organization which had replaced the Comintern—but there was nothing more that he could do to prevent the breakaway.

Stalin had officially disbanded the Comintern because it no longer fulfilled his purpose. In 1947, as an answer to the Marshall Plan, he set up the Cominform—Communist Information—to train agents for overseas propaganda, speed up the pace of socialism in the People's Democracies and unify the work of the communist parties in Western Europe, particularly France and Italy.

During the war many communists, dedicated to the destruction of Nazism, had joined European resistance movements and fought German occupation with exceptional courage. After their countries had been liberated they had taken their places in postwar governments, although they had never managed, outside the communist sphere, to win a majority.

Most statesmen in the West distrusted Soviet intentions. They looked on helplessly while Stalin set up the People's Democracies, and they were aware of the appeal of communist propaganda in countries where people were needy and looking for leadership. The phrase "Cold War" came into use to describe the state of armed neutrality and the bitter battle of words between the Soviet Union and the West. In 1947 President Harry Truman laid down the Truman Doctrine, to assist countries threatened by communist domination. He declared that the United States would go to the aid of any country fighting against communism.

A major source of East-West discord was the existence of a divided Germany. After the war Stalin wanted to strip the whole of Germany bare of machinery, as reparation for the fearful war damage the Nazis had inflicted on the Soviet Union. When the Western nations stopped Stalin's inroads into their zones, he concentrated on Eastern Germany. The Western powers intended to build a democratic state, a Federal Republic of the whole of Germany, but Stalin set up a communist regime in Eastern Germany on a permanent basis. In June 1948 the American, British and French authorities introduced a currency reform in their occupation zones to help put them on a sound financial footing before they regained their independence. The Western powers offered to mint the new money for the Soviet zone as well, but Stalin rejected the new currency for he considered it a cunning move to undermine his control of Eastern Germany.

He replied to the offer by closing the land and water routes to Berlin, hoping to starve the Berliners until they demanded that the American, British and French officials leave the city. But the Western allies refused to submit to Soviet pressure. In a sensational airlift the United States and British air forces supplied the Western sectors of Berlin with the necessities of life for ten months until Stalin accepted defeat. He was able, through the United Nations, to find a way of reopening the routes to Berlin without losing too much face.

In 1949 the communist leader Mao Tse-tung proclaimed the People's Republic of China in Peking, and a communist bloc extended from the frontier of West Germany to the Pacific Ocean. In 1950 a war, which threatened to engulf the world, broke out in the little Far Eastern country of Korea. Equipped with Soviet arms, a North Korean communist army invaded the separate state of South Korea which American forces had occupied after the end of the Second World War and had shortly before evacuated. The South Koreans instantly applied to the United Nations for help. Stalin had miscalculated. He did not think that the United Nations would be able to act or that the Americans would be willing to return. In fact, for three years, a United Nations army—composed mainly of Americans, with contingents from fifteen other member nations—fought along with the South Koreans to stem Russian and Chinese communist aggression. Stalin died four months before a negotiated peace preserved the original frontier between North and South Korea.

Within the Soviet Union industrial progress had been accompanied by a new reign of terror. Stalin was obsessed by fears of rebellion and betrayal to the West, and he imagined every department of government and industry riddled with spies. He opened huge concentration camps and filled them with supposed political offenders. Fresh purges at home and in the People's Democracies created widespread suffering and smothered free thinking. At the same time Stalin revived the persecution of the Russian Orthodox Church, which he had relaxed during the war in order to win the gratitude and undivided loyalty of the nation. He also turned on the victorious Marshals of the Red Army who, he feared, were becoming popular idols and he dismissed them from their commands. He declared that the Party, not the Army, had won the war.

Toward the end of his life Stalin appeared less and less often in public and, shut off behind the forbidding ramparts of the Kremlin, he lost all touch with the outlook of the ordinary people. He became an almost mystical figure, a demigod of communism, Lenin's undisputed heir, ruling by the will of history.

With the iron hand of an absolute dictator, he reduced the position of the Politburo to a mockery. He had always striven for personal power, now he also demanded personal glory. Photographs and portraits of Stalin confronted Soviet citizens at every turn, and he was always presented as a man in the prime of life. The Soviet press and every channel of information was flooded with flattery of Stalin verging on idolatry. *Pravda,* the official journal of the Communist Party, outdid the rest in hysterical expressions of wonder and admiration.

As he grew older Stalin treated the opinions of his colleagues more and more scornfully, and the only politicians who outlived him were those who never questioned his word. From his isolation Stalin failed to grasp the full impact of the changes he himself had brought about in the Soviet Union. Though he had adapted the doctrines of Marx and Lenin to the demands of a modern age, he considered that the people should remain slaves to communism. He could not comprehend that in thirty years a new generation had grown up, and that the average workers were no longer ignorant and illiterate, but citizens of a great industrial power second only to the United States of America. Through hunger, pain and hardship, they had performed a modern miracle. They were proud of their achievement and it was hopeless to try to prevent them from making contact with the outside world. Stalin did not realize that by suppressing original thought he held up progress and defeated his own ends.

On March 5, 1953, Stalin died of a stroke at the age of seventy-three. The news was given out the next day and to most Russians it came as a shock. His personality had loomed over them like a granite monument for so long that it seemed indestructible.

Crowds flocked to the Red Square to see his body carried to the Lenin Mausoleum with immense pomp. The next day the people of Moscow awoke to find Stalin's name displayed side by side with Lenin's, in letters of gold.

11 · *The Downfall of Dictators*

NIKITA KHRUSHCHEV, the latest and perhaps the last of the Russian communist dictators, was born in 1894. He came, like Stalin, of poor peasant stock. His grandfather was a serf and the family lived in a mud hut in a small village on the border of the Ukraine. Nikita had a couple of years of schooling and then worked as a shepherd on a neighboring estate. When he was fifteen his father moved to the Donets Valley to work in the coal mines, because he could not make even a bare living from the land. He always longed to buy a horse, but he could never afford one.

Nikita also went to work in the mines and managed to get a job above ground as a fitter. The pay was bad and the living conditions dreadful. When he first read Karl Marx on the wage system under capitalism, he was convinced that Marx must have known the very mine where he and his father worked.

In his boyhood Khrushchev took little interest in politics. At the outbreak of the October Revolution he joined the Red Guard and a year later became a member of the Party. He was then twenty-four years old. He married early, but his young wife died in the famine of 1920, leaving him with two small children.

Later he married again, very happily, and had a son and two daughters.

The Party was looking for able young men for industry and selected Khrushchev to take a course in the Donets Mining Technical School. He emerged with a sound general education, technical training, and some knowledge of revolutionary theory. After he left the Mining School he took up full-time political work.

The Party tested him on local jobs, and in 1929 summoned him to Moscow to the Industrial Academy. By this time Stalin was in power, and under his leadership Khrushchev gained steady promotion. Though he later denounced the purges and terrorism of these years there is no doubt that he tolerated them at the time, for the slightest sign of opposition would have finished his career. He became head of the Moscow City Committee and among other civic duties completed the building of the magnificent Moscow Metro, the underground railroad system designed to surpass all others in the world.

In 1938 Stalin sent Khrushchev south to take charge of the Ukraine—the largest non-Russian republic—which had a population of forty million and resources vital to the success of the Five Year Plan. It was a most responsible appointment and Khrushchev was in his element. He loved getting things done, and he always preferred working with people rather than ideas— particularly country people, for he was genuinely proud of his peasant background and he understood country ways.

Times had changed since the Lenin-Stalin Declaration of the Rights of the non-Russian Peoples. Their rights had been pared down and they were no longer permitted to preserve their national character. Acting on Stalin's orders, Khrushchev set out to sovietize the Ukrainians by a mixture of argument, intimidation and force. He made Russian the official language, abolished national festivals and revised school history books to exclude Ukrainian heroes and discourage regional patriotism. In 1939 he was appointed a full member of the Politburo.

When the Red Army occupied eastern Poland in September of the same year, Khrushchev was responsible for establishing Soviet rule in the region. He ordered the deportation of trainloads of defenseless Poles to factories in Siberia, and sternly suppressed any sign of Polish nationalism. At the first carefully rigged election, almost 100 per cent of the poll voted communist. Those who might have cast votes for any other party were toiling in Siberia.

In 1941 Nazi armies overran the Ukraine, and for the next three years Khrushchev experienced the full horror of war. He was always near the front line, working with the political commissars, the officers of the Red Army, and the bands of peasant partisans who scorched the earth and harassed the German rearguard. He saw the cities of Kiev and Minsk which he knew and loved reduced to ruins. During the battle of Stalingrad he heard that his eldest son had been killed in the air force.

When the Red Army finally expelled the Germans in 1944 the Ukraine was a scene of death and desolation. It was as if a giant scythe had passed over the land. Soon people began to creep back to live as best they could in caves and dugouts. They had no tools to till the ground, no seed to plant and no house-

Returning to the Ukraine

hold goods of any kind. Often they could not find their own villages because the buildings had been flattened by bombardment and the ruins covered with snow. For a time the United Nations sent UNRRA teams to help the homeless Ukrainians, but it was not long before Khrushchev closed the doors to outside aid in obedience to Stalin's policy of giving the communist countries no cause to be indebted to the West.

Khrushchev did not speak of any change of heart, but he seems to have emerged from the war a different and more humane man. He never again regarded war as a solution to political problems and he had grown closer to the people and further from pure socialist theory. He turned his inexhaustible energy to the task of bringing the Ukraine back to life. In 1950 he was recalled to Moscow and arrived with enthusiasm, and filled with spectacular schemes to reorganize Soviet agriculture. After Stalin died, he worked his way to the forefront of affairs with grim determination. One by one Khrushchev's opponents were deprived of power and some—including Beria, a prominent member of the Politburo—were executed. The precise part played by Khrushchev in these political plots has never been revealed, but his success was sensational and in September 1952 he became First Secretary of the Party.

In 1954 he launched his program for the Virgin Lands of Kazakhstan and southwestern Siberia. On these uncultivated plains Khrushchev planned to plant millions of acres of wheat. He intended to transport two hundred and fifty thousand workers to prepare the land, and to supply them with over a hundred thousand tractors to do the job. He dreamed of colonizing this area with young people, members of the Komsomol—the young Communist League—who, filled with a spirit of adventure and devotion to the Party, would work wonders in the wilderness. As there were no dwellings of any kind, these young "volunteers" were expected to build their own villages and towns in their spare time, and many proved unequal to the task. Khrushchev traveled through the countryside dispelling doubt, raising hope and trying to win people over to his majestic projects.

On February 24, 1956, the Twentieth Party Congress was held in the Kremlin, the first Party Congress since Stalin's death. It turned out to be a momentous occasion and a landmark in the history of Marxism and communism. Nikita Khrushchev, then First Secretary of the Central Committee, and the most powerful man in the Soviet Union, made a secret speech to the assembled company. For three hours he tore to shreds the legend of Stalin's greatness that every Soviet citizen had learned by heart.

Many in his audience must inwardly have questioned the wisdom and justice of Stalin's rule and they probably felt that it was high time to denounce his terrorist acts. But they had not dared protest in his lifetime and after his death they were afraid to admit to any knowledge of the crimes in case they would be held responsible.

The speech was an act of political daring, and could well have destroyed the speaker as well as the image, but Khrushchev had won his way to the top by hard work, a firm belief in the rights of the Russian peasant, and a gift for sizing up new situations. He was perceptive where Stalin had been blind and outgoing where Stalin had been unapproachable.

Khrushchev's main motive in attacking the memory of Stalin was to open the Iron Curtain and let in light from the West. He urged the Russian people to learn from the Western nations in order to overtake them. He realized too that the days when Russians should accept tyrannical government were ending, and that if they became as servile to communism as their ancestors had been to feudal landlords, progress would peter out and the revolution would have been in vain. He encouraged the people to be proud of their progress and he reduced the power of the secret police.

In his speech to the Central Committee Khrushchev charged Stalin with mass cruelty and oppression; with betraying the men who had served him most faithfully; and of establishing a reign of terror. He accused the dead dictator of personal vanity and a lust for self-glorification out of keeping with Marxist principles; of subjecting the will of the Party to his own authority and taking the laws of socialism into his own hands. Finally Khrushchev attacked the fable of Stalin's military genius, his talent for strategy and his infallible foresight, claiming that if Stalin had listened to the warnings of impending Nazi attack he would have been better prepared to meet it. And from his own experience on the Ukraine front, Khrushchev reported that Stalin had compelled experienced generals to take orders from Moscow against their better judgment, with serious consequences.

The actual text of the secret speech was never published inside Russia, but local commissars read a version of it to every provincial council, and people discussed it throughout the length and breadth of the Soviet Union. Khrushchev never contradicted a Western rendering which was published in the world press. He made the speech at a closed session of the Presidium of the Central Committee, but he intended it for world consumption and he did not try to disguise the stand he had taken.

At first the Russian people were stunned to hear the misdeeds of the demigod fearlessly denounced like those of any ordinary man. Death had dulled the sharp edges of discontent and they had come to regard the past tyranny as the unavoidable price of progress. However, as the first shock wore off, the Russians gave up the gilded image of Stalin without too many regrets. It seemed as if a dark cloud had been mysteriously lifted from the Russian skies.

Soon after the speech, Stalin's body was quietly moved from its position of honor beside Lenin, and placed in a grave with a humble headstone by the wall of the Kremlin gardens. Stalin's name was removed from the face of the mausoleum and gradually local authorities renamed their towns and cities, streets, schools, hospitals and libraries. Even Stalingrad, the scene of the triumphant victory, became Volgograd, the city of the Volga River.

Nikita Khrushchev will probably be best remembered by his own people for the part he played in liberating the Soviet Union from the personality cult of Stalinism. His other major achievement was the reshaping of a number of Marxist doctrines, taking into account the discovery of nuclear power and the existence of the Soviet Union. In Marx's day there had been no socialist state, and his belief that universal war was absolutely inevitable and that the evils of capitalism could only be overcome by proletarian violence no longer held true. In Khrushchev's day the Soviet Union was an established fact and powerful enough to challenge "imperialism" by peaceful means. He saw that the hydrogen bomb had changed the whole concept of war, and that a third world war, instead of being a triumph for socialism as Lenin had predicted, would be a total disaster for everyone concerned. No nation could be victorious because the world would be laid waste and civilization would perish. Therefore, in contradiction to the hard and fast theories of more rigid Marxists—particularly Mao Tse-tung—Khrushchev proposed a foreign policy of "peaceful coexistence" between socialist and capitalist countries, and argued that there were other ways of

The spacecraft "Vostok" which carried the first astronaut Yuri Gagarin in 1961

converting people to socialism than by violence.

Khrushchev believed absolutely that socialism leading to communism was the best system of society. But he considered that, since countries like the People's Democracies were on a lower plane of socialist development than the Soviet Union, they should be allowed to work out social change in their own way, always provided that they acknowledged Soviet leadership and recognized Moscow as the capital of world socialism.

He looked toward the newly independent countries of Asia and Africa, then emerging from "imperialist" rule, predicting that communism would gain far more converts among these people by practical results than by intellectual persuasion. Though

Khrushchev attributed the success of the Bolshevik Revolution to the inspiration of Marxism, he reasoned that once a socialist system exists, it must prove its worth by solid economic achievement. He scandalized political idealists at home and abroad by his belief that more people were going to be won over by good harvests and plentiful food supplies than by the *Communist Manifesto*.

He admitted that it might be necessary to make concessions to these African and Asian countries, letting them work toward socialism through what he called "national bourgeois" governments. As they had recently cast off colonial rule they were bound to be anti-imperialist, and it was worthwhile for communist parties to gain a footing among them, always with the object of eventually seizing power.

Khrushchev preferred persuasion to force and he took the job of selling socialism overseas. He pointed out that the success or failure of the communist crusade rested largely on prosperity in the Soviet Union; if men are homeless and hungry, other men are not likely to follow willingly in their footsteps. Khrushchev made grandiose plans for stepping up production and providing people with household goods as well as building up heavy industry. He planned to create confidence at home and attract the uncommitted millions of the world, not only by suspension bridges and power stations, but also by shoes and sewing machines. He dreamed of an ideal communist state where every Russian could live comfortably, dress well and eat plentifully. It is sad that his enthusiasm and imagination so far outran the bounds of possibility that they brought about his downfall.

The Bratsk hydroelectric power station

Khrushchev's attack on Stalin had a disturbing effect on the People's Democracies and they rebelled against the regime that Stalin had imposed on them. In Poland, bloodshed was averted by the leadership of Wladislaw Gomulka, a patriotic Pole who was also a communist. But in Hungary in 1956 Khrushchev crushed an uprising by sending Red Army tanks to shoot down the rebels. It was his last act of open violence, but it left an indelible stain on his reputation as a peacemaker.

He had already begun to take an intense interest in foreign affairs, always with the aim of building up the superiority and security of the Soviet Union. He traveled to Yugoslavia to see Marshal Tito, to China to show his solidarity with Mao Tse-tung, and to India to talk to Prime Minister Nehru. He toured the People's Democracies, attended a summit conference of world statesmen in Geneva, made a dramatic descent on London, and, to the fury of Mao Tse-tung, accepted an invitation from President Dwight D. Eisenhower to visit the United States in 1959. He also attended the Fifteenth Session of the United Nations General Assembly in 1960. These journeys were an outward expression of his growing conviction of the value of "peaceful coexistence" between nations.

He insisted that as the Soviet Union and the United States were the strongest industrial nations in the world, they should bear the main responsibility for preventing another war. Speaking in the Soviet Union he emphatically declared: "Our country and the United States are the two most mighty powers in the world. . . . if war breaks out between America and our country, no one will be able to stop it. It will be a catastrophe on a colossal scale."

In order to prove to Party leaders that he was not deserting the communist camp, and also in order to divert attention from crop failures and industrial confusion at home, he continued to make aggressive speeches, bragging statements and blustering gestures to the leaders of the capitalist countries. Western diplomats were puzzled, confused and worried. They believed that Khrushchev really wanted peace, but they never knew exactly where they stood, or how much they could count on Russian good intentions.

In October 1957 the Russians launched Sputnik I, the first man-made space satellite, and the following year Khrushchev became Premier. He had won mastery of the Soviet Union by a mixture of political cunning and personal courage, and with considerably less bloodshed than his predecessors.

In November 1960 the delegates of eighty-one communist parties assembled in Moscow. They conferred for three weeks and, before they dispersed, signed a document known as the "Moscow Statement" proclaiming their united faith in socialism as "the decisive factor in the development of society," and their conviction that "the complete triumph of socialism is inevitable." The statement acknowledged that the Soviet Union was a step ahead of the rest: "The Soviet Union is successfully carrying on the full-scale construction of a communist society. Other countries of the socialist camp are successfully laying the foundations of socialism. . . ."

The Moscow Statement was a compromise between the convictions of Khrushchev: "The Communist parties of all the world uphold peaceful coexistence . . . and battle resolutely for the prevention of war"; and Mao Tse-tung's inflexible resistance to any contact with the West short of war: "War is a constant companion of capitalism. . . . U.S. imperialism is the main force of aggression and war."

In the closing paragraphs the socialist ranks appeared to be gloriously united: "Marxism-Leninism is a great integral revolutionary doctrine, the guiding light of the working people of the whole world at all stages of their great battle for peace, freedom and a better life, for the establishment of the most just society, communism."

But the road to peace was beset with international crises. In 1960 a U-2, an American reconnaissance aircraft, was shot down over the USSR. When Khrushchev heard the news, he broke off a summit meeting of Western statesmen in Paris and went home livid with indignation at what he termed an American breach of faith. In the following year the precarious peace was shaken once more when the Western powers refused to sign separate peace treaties with East and West Germany. Khrushchev issued an ultimatum giving them six months to sign under threat of war. When the time limit expired he backed down on the use of force. But he ordered a wall to be built around the Soviet zone of Berlin to prevent refugees from escaping the prevailing poverty in East Germany to the more prosperous West. It was a measure of extreme urgency, for about two million enterprising and industrious men and women had already left and East Germany was being drained of initiative and manpower.

But the most dangerous crisis of all arose in October 1962, when, in a desperate attempt to offset failures in the Virgin Lands with a triumph abroad, Khrushchev supplied the communist-ruled island of Cuba with long-range ballistic missiles trained on the United States. News of the impending commu-

Premier Nikita Khrushchev, 1964

nist threat broke on October 22, when a nationwide broadcast from the White House alerted the people that President John F. Kennedy would make a grave statement that same evening. The nation was filled with deep foreboding. The President reported that the Soviet Union was secretly turning the island of Cuba into an armed base. Jet bombers, fitted to carry nuclear warheads, were being assembled on recently constructed airfields, and launching sites for medium- and long-range ballistic missiles had been photographed from the air. The missile sites were directed westward and it appeared that the chief cities of North, Central and Latin America lay within their range. The President spoke firmly without pause or hesitation, announcing that he had sent United States warships to blockade the island and search approaching ships for weapons of war.

In an emergency meeting of the Security Council of the United Nations the situation was debated in anger and fear. Secretary General U Thant warned the Council that "the very existence of mankind is in the balance."

At the same time President Kennedy and Premier Krushchev were in close communication. Though the atmosphere was stormy and the protests bitter on both sides, the two leaders agreed that nuclear war must be avoided at any cost. President Kennedy demanded the withdrawal of all aggressive arms from the island of Cuba and suddenly Khrushchev gave in. Faced by an inflexible ultimatum of armed resistance, he knew when he was beaten. He probably hoped to gain recognition of Soviet strength simply by a show of military might, but he saw that he had miscalculated American reaction, and had only succeeded in bringing the world to the threshold of a third world war. On October 28 Khrushchev agreed to dismantle the Cuban bases and returned to his policy of coexistence.

Khrushchev was greatly troubled by the threatening conflict between his own foreign policy and that of Mao Tse-tung in China. Having decided that the wisest way to establish world communism was to treat with the West, he was terrified that Mao—with his unswerving belief in pure Marxism and inevitable revolution—would provoke the United States into open war. Though he did not at the time inform the West of his decision, Khrushchev refused to give Mao the formula for making the atom bomb, fearing he would use it not only as a deterrent, but also as a weapon of attack. The quarrel between the two communist leaders smoldered under the mask of eternal friendship until, in 1962, Mao brought it into the open by claiming the leadership of the socialist movements in Asia, Africa and Latin America.

In the newly independent countries of Asia and Africa, Khrushchev had resolved to gain control by political propaganda bolstered by overwhelming proof of Soviet prosperity. The people were hungry and he offered them food, the governments were inexperienced and he offered them a program backed up by loans of money and teams of technicians to carry it out. It was an immense field for communist conquest and he could not possibly surrender it to a rival leader.

Once the quarrel with China was out in the open, Khrushchev and Mao constantly reviled each other in their speeches and writings. The Western world was at first mystified and then relieved by the split in communist ranks. It added considerably to Khrushchev's anxieties, because he had to calculate the effect of his every political move, not only on the West, but also on a powerful enemy close at hand.

In 1964 Khrushchev's colleagues, most of whom owed their positions to him, turned against him. They were frightened at the immensity of his development schemes, and the breakneck speed with which he set out to operate them. The development of the Virgin Lands had not come up to expectations, and the countless acres of corn he had insisted on planting on land where corn had never grown before, and evidently never could grow, had been an expensive failure. Also they resented his growing authority, and were afraid that he might give up too much to come to an understanding with the capitalist West. They suspected he might even have dealings with the heads of big business in West Germany.

In the autumn of 1964, while Khrushchev was on a holiday at his villa on the Black Sea, the members of the Presidium made up their minds. They carefully prepared their case against Khrushchev and summoned him to Moscow on an excuse of urgent business. When he appeared, the commissars presented their charges one after the other. They accused him of treachery, extravagance and despotism.

Khrushchev stubbornly defended his actions and his aims. He upheld his policy of representing the Soviet Union at the summit conferences of the Western world. Although he admitted that he had been forced to sacrifice the material welfare of the people to a massive arms program and a leading position in the space race, he pointed out that whenever it came to a showdown he had stopped in time. Although he had talked of war, he had always stood for peace. He claimed to have freed the Russian people from internal tyranny and terror. Moreover, he was convinced that the immense economic projects which he had introduced would pay off in the end. The Presidium was not impressed. They demanded his resignation, but Khrushchev refused to accept their verdict. He appealed to the members of the Central Committee of the Communist Party for support. When they voted against him, he acknowledged defeat and agreed to hand in his resignation.

The process of Khrushchev's dismissal is perhaps his best memorial. He was voted out of office by general consent, but he was neither executed nor exiled. In ten years he had raised the standard of political behavior in the Soviet Union. Though he was by no means blameless in his treatment of political adversaries, he had altered the outlook on violence, denounced the purges and discontinued them. When he was forced out of office Western leaders hoped that some of his plans for better understanding with the United States, France and Britain would be adopted by his successors. He had great technical success, for he saw Russian astronauts launched in space, and he brought home to the leaders of the Soviet Union the danger of nuclear war. This could be counted an important step in the direction of peace.

12 · From the Manchus to Mao Tse-tung

SEVEN HUNDRED MILLION PEOPLE, about a quarter of the population of the entire world, live in the People's Republic of China. They are heirs to a magnificent civilization, and the founders of socialism in the Far East.

While Russia was in the throes of violent revolution, imperial rule in China was also crumbling away. For more than three thousand years the Chinese had reigned supreme among Asian peoples, secure in the belief that they possessed a superior culture, and immensely proud of their traditional way of life. Protected by the Great Wall of China, a succession of majestic emperors—honored by their subjects as Sons of Heaven—ruled in haughty ignorance of the outside world.

In the nineteenth century foreign nations shattered this lordly seclusion and shook the foundations of Chinese sovereignty. It was an age of scientific and political awakening. The United States discovered enormous riches within its territory and became a powerful nation; Japan emerged from two hundred years of feudal isolation and excelled in industry; Russia began to take a hand in Far Eastern affairs; and all over Europe new inventions speeded up production and transport and changed the

The Great Wall of China

way of life. While many other nations turned from manpower to machines and from candlelight to electricity, Chinese rulers savagely resisted any form of change and continued to live as they had in the past.

But they fought a losing battle. European merchants were looking for new markets and they arrived in Chinese ports with cargoes of manufactured goods to trade for tea, cotton and silk. The British led the way and caused great harm by first introducing a taste for opium and then selling the drug at huge profit. Imports of opium were forbidden, and the Chinese protested violently, destroyed the incoming cargoes, and finally went to war against the British. But they were defeated and the opium trade continued.

A dynasty of Manchu emperors had held the throne since the mid-seventeenth century. They had treated foreign travelers with condescension, referring to them as "barbarians," uncivilized outsiders, who came simply to pay homage or tribute. The Manchus were scandalized when representatives of foreign governments approached the Chinese as equals, demanding trade treaties and facilities to develop the country. Anti-foreign demonstrations broke out in many cities, and the general unrest was intensified by frequent rebellions against the declining efficiency and growing corruption of Manchu rule.

The climax came in 1894 when China went to war with Japan over the possession of the country of Korea, which had long been a Chinese vassal state. In less than a year the vast Chinese empire suffered a swift, decisive defeat by her smaller, but much better armed and disciplined, neighbor. The Chinese people were deeply humiliated and their weakness was revealed to the world. It was suddenly evident that the Manchus could not put up any serious opposition and foreign powers tightened their hold on the failing empire. The British controlled most of the foreign trade and the customs system. With the French, German and other European nations, they obtained land concessions and special privileges for their resident officials. The Russians built the Trans-Siberian Railway from Moscow to the Pacific port of Vladivostok and negotiated an agreement to lay the last six hundred miles of line across the Chinese province of Manchuria. This engineering enterprise, like many others, increased foreign political power in China.

But, by this time, anger was mixed with curiosity and, impressed by tales of Western progress, Chinese students began to go to universities in the United States and Japan. They absorbed new ideas and brought them home. The Manchus opposed any kind of change but they could not stop it. In 1911 the reigning empress died, leaving a boy emperor and an incompetent regent to govern the country. Already a young reformer named Sun Yat-sen was working with other revolutionary leaders to stir up rebellion. Insurrections broke out and city after city declared against the Manchus. In 1912 the young emperor abdicated and a republic was proclaimed with Sun Yat-sen as the first president.

In the following decade China was torn by political rivalry and military strife. It was customary for the governors of the various provinces to raise private armies to keep order in their own realms. They were warlords, successors to the robber barons of old, constantly fighting among themselves for greater power and changing sides whenever it suited them.

Religious influence had gradually declined and the teachings of Confucius, the learned sage and social reformer whose doctrines had set the standard of public and private behavior for over two thousand years, had lost their unifying force. Confucius strove to create national harmony and world order through true goodness and human understanding. He named truth, wisdom, kindness and courage the finest virtues; and he believed in family life as the basis of civilization. He taught children to honor their parents and the spirits of their ancestors who he told them were always present. He was convinced that the example of a happy home would spread to the community, the country and finally to society as a whole. Confucius' family was poor and he was largely self-taught, but he had a profound admiration for education. His teaching promoted family loyalty and a respect for scholarship. But by the twentieth century many ancestral laws had lost their meaning and people who looked to them for protection and guidance found a void. So they turned for comfort and inspiration to the compelling creeds of a modern age and listened to the voices of nationalism, socialism and communism.

In 1921 Sun Yat-sen was elected president of a Nationalist government, known as the Kuomintang, with headquarters in Canton in southern China. In the same year the Chinese Communist Party was founded in Shanghai by a small group of intellectuals, including an ardent young revolutionary named Mao Tse-tung. Sun pictured China, not in the traditional way as a boundless center of spiritual and cultural power, but as a single nation with fixed frontiers. Mao, on the other hand, pictured the Chinese people as the champions of perpetual revolution and social reform in a classless world. Both men were confident that their countrymen were superior to other peoples simply because they were Chinese.

The Kuomintang founded a Military Academy at Whampoa, near Canton, and the Russians supplied advisers, arms and money to train a Chinese Red Army. In 1925 Sun Yat-sen died and his chief military aide, Chiang Kai-shek, formed a government which included communist members.

However, despite direct support from Stalin, Chiang soon turned against the Russian Communist Party in order to win the support of the Western nations, for he felt they were richer and more reliable than the Soviet Union. He seized an insurrection in Shanghai as an excuse for a savage massacre. The Chinese Marxists had tried to follow the Bolshevik example by starting revolution in the cities, but there was so little industry that the proletariat was too weak to win. Thousands of revolutionaries died in Shanghai alone, and respect for Stalin and Russian communism waned. Mao Tse-tung led the battered remnants of the Party to a secret hideout in his home province of Hunan. He began to see that the social scene in China was different from that in Russia and to wonder if the same rules for revolution worked from country to country.

Mao had been born in 1893 in a fairly prosperous peasant home where the family raised pigs and rice. His mother was a devout Buddhist who brought her son up in the same faith until his adolescence when he cast aside religious belief. Mao was a restless and rebellious boy, consumed with curiosity about men's beliefs, and filled with a desire for knowledge. When his father took him out of school at the age of thirteen to work in the rice fields, he ran away from home and went from school to school, seeking some master creed to satisfy his ideals. He studied revolutionary theory and in 1920, at the age of twenty-seven, he read the first Chinese translation of the *Communist Manifesto*. In his autobiography he wrote that from this moment he considered himself a Marxist.

From his rough headquarters in the mountains of Hunan Mao reviewed his meager forces. Deliberating on the communist defeat in Shanghai, he decided that in a country like China, where factory workers were a tiny minority, revolution and social change could only be accomplished through the strength of the peasant masses. He put his conclusions into vivid words: "The force of the peasants is like raging winds and driving rain. It is rapidly increasing in violence. No force can stand in its way. . . . The broad masses of the peasantry have arisen to fulfill their historic destiny."

But Mao saw too that sheer revolt was not enough. It had to be directed, organized and harnessed to the communist cause; otherwise it would come to nothing. At this point he had very little military experience, but he gradually evolved the strategy which eventually made him the master of China. He saw that an army needed something inspiring to fight for, discipline in the face of danger, and the friendship of the peasants as their land became a battlefield.

Former armies had stormed through the Chinese country-side, leaving desolation, hunger and hatred. Mao commanded his troops to take nothing from the peasants that they did not pay for. He recruited partisans, wherever his Red Army rested, and if he was forced to withdraw he left them arms and cadres— trained political agents—to keep alive the spirit of rebellion. The guerrilla, or partisan, bands handled supplies, kept communications open and freed the regular soldiers for combat. Mao also promised the peasants long-overdue land reforms. Under the Manchus large properties were owned by absentee landlords who received the profits of the harvest in good years and took little interest in the fate of their tenant farmers when the crops failed. Destitute peasants fell into the hands of crafty moneylenders who made money by keeping them constantly in debt and penury.

In Hunan Mao formed his first Chinese communist state, but, surrounded by Chiang's Nationalist forces, he found it too insecure for a permanent capital. In 1934 he determined to escape northward to an impregnable mountain bastion where he could lay the firm foundations of Communist China.

This was the famous Long March which established Mao as an almost legendary figure in China. He sent orders to his Red Army commanders and they set out, approximately eighty thousand strong, to break through the Nationalist ring. Three hundred and sixty-eight days later, twenty thousand survivors arrived in the province of Shensi. Mao has never given an account of the Long March, but other writers have calculated the distance and decided that the Red Army traveled six thousand miles, fighting most of the way; crossed eighteen mountain ranges and twenty-four major rivers; and escaped capture by twelve warlords. It is an almost unrecorded epic of resolve, endurance and good battle tactics. In Yenan, Mao set up a capital far from interference by the Nationalist forces of Chiang Kai-shek and in touch with the Soviet Union. This is a policy Mao has preached to would-be revolutionaries in under-developed countries ever since, urging their leaders to set up communist capitals, separate from the established seats of government, headquarters for a war of liberation.

While the Chinese were waging civil war, the Japanese had been edging into the Chinese province of Manchuria. In less than a hundred years they had progressed from feudalism to

The ancient gateway to Yenan

capitalism and rivaled the most advanced nations of the West in industrial achievement. But they were overcrowded in their narrow islands and desperately short of raw materials. The vast, unexploited Chinese mainland was a tempting prize. In 1937 they moved into Manchuria, and China declared war. Chiang Kai-shek and Mao Tse-tung were forced to sink their political differences for the common cause and they united against the common enemy. But the alliance was fraught with difficulties; neither faction was prepared to take orders from rival commanders and they never fought against the Japanese as a national army.

In 1939 the Second World War broke out; and in 1941 Japanese carrier-borne aircraft attacked the United States naval base of Pearl Harbor and the Second World War spread to the Pacific. Supplied with American arms Chiang Kai-shek, now promoted to the rank of Generalissimo, took over the official command of the Chinese forces and eventually shared in the Allied victory over Japan.

Once the foreign aggressor was defeated, the uneasy alliance between Chinese Communists and Nationalists foundered. In July 1946 civil war broke out all over China, and Mao announced the formation of the People's Liberation Army. Official figures are lacking, but it is estimated that he had well over a million men under his command, and an arsenal of Japanese weapons he had collected in Manchuria with Soviet consent. Chiang Kai-shek had cut down his forces, but still retained about three million men and a large stock of American war material.

In the first year of civil war the Nationalists were victorious everywhere and the Red Army fell back. But in the summer of 1947 Mao changed his tactics. He avoided head-on battles and kept his men as a mobile force, never attacking except at the spots where he had superior strength. By good leadership and clever propaganda he won over Nationalist soldiers, trained them in Red Army discipline and doctrines, and set up Communist centers in conquered country. The war continued all through 1948 with heavy casualties on both sides. Gradually Chiang Kai-shek's forces were weakened by dissension among the generals and desertion in the ranks, while morale in the People's Army of Liberation was high.

THE LONG MARCH

U. S. S. R.

MONGOLIAN
REPUBLIC

GREAT WALL

Harbin
MANCHURIA   Vladivostok

N. KOREA   JAPAN

Peking Tientsin
SHENSI
Yenan Hwang-ho

S. KOREA   Tokyo

TIBET   C   H   I   N   A   Nanking

Yangtze
Shanghai

HUNAN

INDIA

Juichin

FORMOSA
(TAIWAN)

BURMA

Canton

Hanoi   Hongkong   PACIFIC OCEAN

N. VIETNAM

LAOS

THAILAND

PHILIPPINE
REPUBLIC

CAMBODIA   S. VIETNAM

Saigon

0 Miles   400

China and the Far East today

Mao left the Nationalist-occupied cities to the last. By this
time his forces outnumbered the enemy. He surrounded the
cities one by one, cut their communications and reduced them

to the point of surrender. When he reached the banks of the Yangtze River some of his advisers were in favor of calling a halt and making a pact with the Nationalists. But Mao was determined to press on to final victory, a decision of supreme importance in the annals of Chinese Communism. He has preached to his own people and to communist converts in Asia, Africa and Latin America that there should never be any compromise or half measures. The Marxist-capitalist struggle is a war to the death.

On October 1, 1949 Mao Tse-tung triumphantly proclaimed the People's Republic of China in Peking. Chiang Kaishek withdrew from the mainland to the off-shore island of Formosa (Taiwan) where he set up a Nationalist Government, claiming that it was the rightful government of all China.

The communist countries enthusiastically recognized Red China. The British followed their official tradition of accepting the representative governments of other nations whether they agree with their politics or not. In the course of time most European and many Asian and African countries followed suit.

The United States had supplied Chiang Kai-shek with arms and ammunition during the Second World War, in order to prevent China from being overrun by Japanese armies. They supported him against Mao Tse-tung throughout the civil war and when he was driven to Formosa they continued to recognize him as the only legal ruler. The United States Government regards Mao Tse-tung and his fellow communists as rebels and warmongers. It has consistently refused to recognize the People's Republic of China as a legal government and has opposed its membership in the United Nations. With American financial aid and the help of the United Nations agencies, Formosa has become an orderly, prosperous state; but Chiang Kai-shek has never given up the idea of winning back control of the mainland.

Mao proved himself an outstanding leader. He became Chairman of the People's Republic and set out to repair the ravages of war and build the country of his dreams. His followers adopted his interpretation of Marxism-Leninism as the basic guide for the future. The Party accepted "perpetual revolution" and the establishment of "socialism and communism in China" as a sacred duty and a destiny. Western leaders who had hoped that Mao would content himself with much-needed land reform and stamping out corruption were doomed to disappointment. It soon became clear that revolution in China was even more sweeping than in Russia, and that Mao was the most extreme Marxist of all the communist leaders.

13 · Red China

MAO HAD AN ENORMOUS FUND of manpower at his disposal to repair the war damage within the People's Republic, and to keep up the strength of the Red Army. But he did not have either the money or machines to do the job. In December 1949 he accepted an invitation from Stalin to visit Moscow, hoping to cement the friendship between the two great communist states and to secure financial and industrial aid. He arrived at the Kremlin just in time to take part in the elaborate celebrations in honor of Stalin's seventieth birthday. To Mao the festivities must have seemed out of keeping with the guiding principles of a truly socialist state, and it is possible that later in life, when he decried the Soviet system of government, he had the sumptuous birthday repasts at the back of his mind.

For many years Stalin had backed Chiang Kai-shek and looked down on Mao as an unimportant adventurer. But the Soviet dictator had lately been defeated by the Western powers in their Berlin airlift and he could not afford to ignore a brand-new ally in the East. He gave Mao red-carpet treatment and greeted him with every sign of respect. The discussions between the two leaders lasted for two months and undoubtedly covered a wide range of mutual interests. Foremost among them was the thorny problem of Manchuria, which Stalin had stripped bare of machinery after the Japanese retreat, in the same way that he had stripped East Germany. Manchuria is Chinese territory, and at that time it was the only industrial area in the whole country, and Mao urgently needed the factories in working order. Finally Stalin agreed to replace the stolen material and send Soviet technicians to build new factories and teach the Chinese how to use them. Before Mao left Moscow in February 1950 he announced for all the world to hear that the link between Moscow and Peking was "eternal and indestructible."

In June 1950 the Korean War broke out. There is no evidence to show how much voice Mao had in the original plan, or indeed if Stalin had told him ahead of time his intention to induce the North Koreans to invade South Korea. Faced with the heavy task of reconstruction at home, Mao was probably very reluctant to commit himself to a war against the United States or any other nation. It is likely that if he heard of the project at all, he agreed with Stalin that the Americans would take no action to protect South Korea and that the war would soon be over. However, by the end of 1950 the North Korean Army was retreating in disorder and the United Nations armies were approaching the Chinese frontier. Then Mao flung the best units of his Red Army into Korea. They fought with fanatical courage and bore tremendous losses until July 1953 when an armistice was signed confirming the prewar boundary between North and South Korea. The United Nations forces were satisfied that they had stemmed the tide of communist aggression, though

Mao claimed outright victory. He continued to send Chinese communist guerrillas to Malaya, Indonesia, the frontiers of India and other Far Eastern countries to harass the newly independent "national bourgeois" governments and set alight liberation movements. Most of these guerrilla bands were slowly and painfully hunted down in savage jungle warfare by local troops and regiments of the British Army. In 1950 Mao invaded Tibet, and in the following year signed an agreement which virtually deprived the Tibetans of independant government. This policy of communist infiltration came to an ugly head in the formerly French possession of Vietnam, where a revolutionary movement developed into a full-scale war with North Vietnamese forces and the Vietcong (South Vietnamese communists), supplied with Chinese and Russian arms, fighting against South Vietnamese forces supported by a substantial number of American troops and contingents from Australia, New Zealand and South Korea.

Meanwhile Mao was building a socialist state at home. Though he did not stage public purges with mock trials and confessions on Stalin's scale, there is no doubt that he speedily eliminated any troublemakers who opposed his regime. In the early days he, like Lenin, encouraged the peasants with promises of land and urged them to seize it by force. The death rate was lower than in Russia only because most of the landlords lived in the cities and the peasants could not reach them. This private peasant ownership was a passing phase, for Mao soon began to plan collective farms on the Soviet pattern. He carried out collectivization with less bloodshed and violence than in Russia, but in the end it was even more comprehensive. By 1957 all the

Red Army soldiers build a road

land except small garden plots had been transferred to collective farms, and the peasants' dreams of possessing their own property were shattered.

Mao offered Chinese businessmen a temporary interest in their own concerns while the government was in the process of taking them over. If they agreed they became cogs in the communist machine; if they refused they were instantly executed.

In 1953 he launched the first Five Year Plan, and described it as a gradual transition to socialism. Government bodies worked with the Party, and the Party was always in control. Mao clearly stated his long-term policy, "to advance steadily under the leadership of the working class and the Communist Party, from an agricultural to an industrial country, from a new democratic to a classless society, to abolish classes and achieve world socialism."

In 1958 Mao announced the second Five Year Plan with a fanfare of propaganda. He heralded it as The Great Leap Forward, and set fantastic goals for the long-suffering peasants. By this time Khrushchev had come to power and the crack in Chinese and Russian solidarity was beginning to show. It could be that Mao intended, with The Great Leap Forward, to overtake Soviet achievement and discredit Soviet leaders who he considered had become soft and satisfied with their system of government.

As The Great Leap Forward got under way, collective farms were turned into communes—self-supporting units which were supposed to provide from their own resources all the needs of a community. The seventy or eighty thousand people of a single commune were directed to irrigate the land and farm it, build roads and bridges, construct factories and produce their own tools, and, most important of all, balance their budgets. They were provided with communal nurseries so that mothers could leave their children and go out to work, and public recreation rooms where everyone received continuous political education. As a first step toward pure communism, free supplies of food and clothing were handed out to compensate for low wages. The communes were intended to strengthen socialism at the expense of family life, destroy the last links with Confucianism, and bridge the gap between socialism and the classless society.

Mao did not permit the details of any reverses to reach the outside world, and accurate figures of progress inside Red China are hard to obtain. But from year to year foreign observers have formed an idea of the food situation in China from the amount of grain that Mao has had to buy abroad. It appeared that the communes had a disastrous effect on the country. For three years production fell, harvests failed, and matters were made worse by widespread floods. Enterprises like the "backyard furnaces," from which peasants were expected to produce enough steel for all their requirements, closed down because the steel was of such poor quality that it would not stand the stresses of modern machinery. News leaked out that the most rigid regulations of the communes had to be relaxed.

In 1959 Mao resigned as head of state, although he retained the all-powerful post of Chairman of the Party. From this time onward he devoted more time to foreign affairs. From the early days of the People's Republic he had begun to challenge Soviet leadership of the communist parties in the Asian and African countries recently liberated from European colonial rule, such as: India, which was formerly British; Indonesia, formerly Dutch; Vietnam, formerly French; and the Congo, formerly Belgian. He acknowledged the Bolshevik Revolution as the first great liberation movement in a capitalist country, the forerunner of social liberty. But he tried to exclude Soviet influence from the Far East, and claimed that the Chinese revolutionary war was the perfect pattern for all future liberation movements in Asia, Africa, and also in Latin America. Mao admitted that the Russians had freed themselves from their local capitalist oppressors, but boasted that the Chinese, by their refusal to have dealings with any "imperialist" country, had gone further along the road to pure communism and freed themselves from the capitalists of the whole world.

When Khrushchev advocated coexistence Mao stepped up his attack and abandoned all pretense of friendship. He used the word "revisionism" as a term of bitter abuse to describe the Russian behavior. According to Mao, revisionists are communists who have betrayed the sacred communist cause. He claims that because they have discarded true revolutionary doctrines, abandoned the ideal of perpetual revolution in favor of a semi-socialist peaceful existence, they have become United States stooges and are beneath contempt. He despised and condemned Khrushchev's policy of persuasion and of selling socialism gradually by an exhibition of prosperity. Instead he tempted Asian and African leaders with the prospect of a rapid rise to power through armed revolution, and denied that Chinese and Russian Communists had anything in common at all. In reply Khrushchev recalled the technicians who were working in China and left hundreds of factories half finished. But this was a small price to pay for permanent revolution, and Mao was convinced that if many millions of Chinese had to die in the struggle for world communism, the survivors would carry on until final victory. He regarded war as "the highest form of revolution," a hardener of character, and he regretted that the younger generation in the People's Republic was growing up without experiencing the stress of battle.

In the summer of 1966 Mao, aging and perhaps ill, staged what he termed a "cultural revolution" to cleanse the Party

Children in training for the cultural revolution

organization of the Chinese People's Republic of evil influences. It seems that he resolved, through widespread havoc, to restore the conditions of violent change and revive the sense of urgency which had spurred the early Chinese communists on to victory. It was evident that some of the Party leaders fell short of Marxist ideals and they did not share to the full Mao's passion for austerity and struggle. He was terrified that when he died the country would sink back into a kind of semi-capitalism where people worked for personal profit and enjoyed peaceful pastimes. It is evident from official pronouncements that Mao hoped through the shock of the cultural revolution to reset the standards of political thought and eliminate all unworthy candidates for the succession.

Mao wanted also to inject a fresh spirit into the Red Army, for he feared that the officers and men were not as political-minded as they had been, and that they were becoming too independent of the Party. Again and again he abused Soviet revisionism as a horrible example of a socialist state that had run to seed.

First and foremost in his campaign for chaos Mao set out to get the young people on his side, to stir up enthusiasm for adventure and give them an exciting job to do. In the opening phase of the cultural revolution he closed the schools and universities so that every student could take part in a countrywide revolt against law and order. He enrolled boys and girls between the ages of twelve and twenty-two in a Red Guard, and provided them with guns, banners and arm bands. He sent them off on "Long Marches" with *The Thoughts of Mao Tse-tung* strapped to their knapsacks, and encouraged them to run riot. At the

Absorbing the Thoughts of Mao Tse-tung

same time Mao formed the Red Rebel Revolutionary Workers'
Organization from older "volunteers," thus adding to the general confusion.

Lawlessness prevailed. The Red Guards stormed through
the country wrecking property, sabotaging factories and disrupting public services. The peasants were too busy with political
demonstrations to look after their land and neglected the spring
sowing so that food stocks ran low. Trains were delayed and
raw materials did not reach the factories. An unknown number

of people were killed and injured in armed clashes and thousands of homes destroyed. In the British island colony of Hong Kong, pro-Peking rioters caused considerable damage and many deaths.

Although there were no sweeping political purges or mass executions, Chinese leadership underwent perceptible changes. Liu Shao-chi, who had been head of state since Mao resigned the position in 1959, appeared on glaring wall posters as China's most dangerous public enemy. He was succeeded as Mao's heir apparent by Lin Piao, the Minister of Defense who had given his blessing and support to the cultural revolution. Chou En-lai, who had played a large part in the original Long March and had served as Premier since the foundation of the Chinese People's Republic, gradually lost his authority. He had tried to preserve an appearance of national unity despite mounting political strife and his attitude was too moderate for Mao's fiery program.

News from China is strictly censored and it is difficult to sift truth from speculation, but by the summer of 1967, it appeared that after a year of cultural revolution, many Chinese had grown tired of the wanton destruction, and angered by the outrageous behavior of the Red Guards. Peking and the surrounding area remained obedient to Mao's commands, but in the provinces military leaders took the law into their own hands and tried to restore order. The industrial city of Wuhan, in southwest China, became a center of resistance to Peking policy. Mao dared not take too strong a hand in suppressing Wuhan defiance because a great bridge across the Yangtze River lay in Wuhan territory and the destruction of the bridge would affect the economy of the entire republic.

Military commanders in other provinces opposed Red Guard action and for a time it looked as if civil war might once more divide China. But the fighting died down, the cultural revolution came to a ragged end, and in the autumn of 1967 Mao still held an unrivaled position. When the schools reopened it was reported from reliable sources that the pupils returned reluctantly to their desks and that the teachers found it difficult to reestablish discipline.

Mao Tse-tung won his way to power by exceptional skill in military strategy, an appreciation of the power of the vast peasant population, and, above all, by his intellectual leadership. He is a politician, a philosopher and a poet, a soldier and a statesman. His character is a blend of idealism and cunning. Both his admirers and his critics find it difficult to understand how a great love of beauty can go hand in hand with utter ruthlessness. He has the ability to analyze Marxist theory and the will to put it into practice. There is no question of his pride in the Chinese people and faith in their destiny. Moreover, he has the talent to translate his convictions into impressive words. As soon as a Chinese child can read, he or she receives a copy of *The Thoughts of Mao Tse-tung* as a lifelong companion and guide.

Mao believes that mass idealism can accomplish miracles, and he considers every citizen of the People's Republic invincible because they are armed with his Thought. Poster propaganda is a striking feature in Red China. It is one of the many expressions of Mao's emphasis on the power of united thinking. He has always considered it important to make a direct appeal to the masses, even if it results in chaos, for they can learn only through

A poster portrait of Mao Tse-tung

conflict and strife. In Peking alone thousands of giant posters appear each week, proclaiming what Mao wants the people to know, and feel and believe. He cannot be sure that they all read the newspapers, but no one can fail to be struck by the posters at every street corner. Their visual impact is irresistible. They are pro-Marx, pro-Mao, pro-perpetual struggle for struggle's sake, pro-the recently developed hydrogen bomb and every other Chinese triumph. They are anti-Russian, anti-the United States, anti-compromise and contentment, and anti-the revisionist Chinese officials whom Mao suspects of straying from the narrow path of pure Marxism.

Mao Tse-tung is a perplexing person. To hundreds of millions of Chinese he is almost godlike. To most of the rest of the world he seems a dangerous and powerful fanatic, and Red China has few friends among other nations.

In the end he will undoubtedly be judged by the social and economic success or failure within the People's Republic of China and by the performance of Red China in the community of nations.

To his followers his sayings are sacred. One of the most familiar and the most frightening runs: "Every communist must grasp the truth; political power grows out of the barrel of a gun."

14 · *Marxism and Communism Today*

IN NOVEMBER 1967 COMMUNISTS in many countries celebrated the fiftieth anniversary, the golden jubilee, of the October Revolution. (The day now falls in November because after the revolution the Russians changed their calendar to fit in with international dates.) Moscow and other communist capitals were scenes of mass rejoicing. Party leaders proclaimed a national three-day holiday throughout the Soviet Union, a luxury unheard of since the Bolsheviks came to power. In the Kremlin a massive bronze statue of Lenin was ceremoniously unveiled. On November 6, in the Red Square, more than two million Russians marched in a jubilee parade to display communist achievement and Soviet might. With banners flying to the beat of martial music and the stirring strains of the "Internationale," units of the armed forces, members of the trade unions, athletes and astronauts, representatives of the fifteen Soviet republics and many trades saluted Communist Party leaders who stood in the place of honor on Lenin's mausoleum. Riders in Cossack uniforms, mounted on prancing white horses, recalled the Russian past, and huge ballistic weapons demonstrated the nuclear power of the Soviet Union in the present. Everywhere giant portraits of Lenin dominated the celebrations.

1967—Moscow celebrates the Fiftieth Anniversary of the October Revolution

Shortly before the anniversary Leonid Brezhnev, Secretary of the Soviet Communist Party, had summoned world communist leaders to a conference in the Kremlin to confirm communist aims and demonstrate Soviet Party leadership. Most heads of communist states went to Moscow, but there were several important absentees. Mao Tse-tung did not reply to the invitation, Fidel Castro of Cuba sent his minister of health as a substitute, and no Albanian communist leader was present. Meanwhile, in the noncommunist countries philosophers and politicians, historians and economists, scientists and sociologists tried to analyze the development of Marxism and assess its impact on social conditions today.

Marx molded his theories into a missionary creed to convert the world to a belief in social equality through violent revolution. But though Marxism spread far from the country of its origin, it has not fulfilled the dreams or, in day-to-day practice, supported the basic theories of its founder.

Lenin was an ardent Marxist, but he was the first communist leader to admit that in industry complete economic equality was not a workable proposition. He found it impossible to run a progressive economy without a profit motive, and saw the need for a stimulus and the promise of "better work more pay" to speed up production. The principle of "for each according to his needs" is simply not acceptable to the expert in any trade. In the Soviet Union the difference between the wages of an average unskilled laborer and a skilled worker has persisted, and if anything increased. Since the days of Stalin's first Five Year Plan factory managers have received large cash bonuses for efficiency in fulfilling their orders. Present Party leaders are moving even further from Marxist theory by giving managers a chance to plan their own production instead of working on hard and fast instructions from a central office in Moscow. These new concessions mean that heads of firms are able to fit supply to demand. They not only give people the goods they want, but also make more profit.

Marx was mistaken too in his expectation that revolution would break out first in Germany, France or Britain, the most industrialized countries of Western Europe. He dismissed Russia somewhat contemptuously as a backward eastern land, a citadel of imperialism, populated by a mass of illiterate peasants unable and unworthy to carry his revolutionary message to the waiting world. In fact, most communist revolutions have come about in industrially backward countries with large peasant populations.

Marx's third miscalculation lay in his conviction that once revolution began it would spread with irresistible force, uniting factory workers in a mighty proletarian movement and sweeping away the barriers—not only of class but also of nationality. He thought it inevitable that individual states would lose their importance and wither away.

It now seems that the vision of Marxism fighting for a universal classless society may be defeated by the passionate forces of nationalism fighting for separate, independent states. At the end of the Second World War, Western leaders recognized Eastern Europe as a Soviet sphere of interest, and they saw that they could not restrain the Russians from setting up communist regimes by armed force. To begin with, communism won some voluntary support from people who were destitute and looking for leadership, but the spirit of nationalism soon proved stronger. Far from withering away under a communist regime, the state has become the mainstay of the social system. As Party and state are inseparable, the success of the Party depends on the internal power of the state administration.

In the People's Democracies of Poland, Hungary, Czechoslovakia, Yugoslavia, Albania, Rumania, Bulgaria and, above all, East Germany, Russian leaders have tried unsuccessfully to wipe out nationalism and replace it with communism.

East Germany is one of the cornerstones of the Russian communist structure. The Russians argue that the future security of the Soviet Union depends on the permanent separation of

The People's Democracies of Eastern Europe

East and West Germany, because West Germany alone can never be powerful enough to attack the Soviet bloc. Furthermore Russian leaders are constantly predicting that social conditions will worsen in the West and that the whole of Germany will turn communist. The other People's Democracies are striving in their various ways to attain economic independence and preserve national traditions. But they accept Soviet division of Germany as a safeguard against a third world war.

Although the people of the satellite states have different historical backgrounds, they show similar symptoms of nationalism. Very few were Russian-speaking when the Bolsheviks came to power, and none have changed their language since. All desired self-government and resented the authority of Party leaders trained in Moscow. They also objected to Soviet pressure which forced them to sell their produce at poor prices, and in return purchase goods at high Soviet-set rates.

Marshal Tito, President of Yugoslavia, was the first head of a People's Democracy to defy Kremlin leadership. A convinced communist, but a nationalist at heart, Tito refused to sacrifice the interests of his own people to the interests of the Soviet Union. In 1948 he openly declared that Yugoslavia would retain the right to treat with governments outside the Soviet orbit, and practice an independent form of communism geared to the character and needs of the Yugoslav people.

When Stalin died in 1953 people in the satellite states felt that an era of iron repression had ended and grasped at a chance of winning greater freedom. In East Germany smoldering indignation turned into open rebellion, sternly suppressed by armed force. When Khrushchev made his speech condemning Stalin, renewed hope spurred the nationalists into action. In 1956 anti-Russian revolution broke out in Hungary and industrial riots erupted in Poland. The Hungarian patriots were defeated by Russian armies, but they still gained some concessions. The Poles won more concrete benefits. Wladyslaw Gomulka, a Polish communist who had been imprisoned for nationalist views, was released and allowed to return to political life. He was elected secretary of the Party and under his guidance the Poles have dissolved the hated collective farms and permitted the existence of the Roman Catholic Church. At the same time they continue to follow the Kremlin line in foreign policy. They are in their public pronouncements pro-Russian and anti-West.

Early in 1968 a new wave of protest and desire for freedom of expression arose among Polish students. Gomulka tried hard to keep a middle course between the young demonstrators and the conventional Party leaders. But the Party succeeded in putting down the disturbances and, as some rebellious students and supporters of liberalism were Jewish, their demands were followed by widespread repression of Polish Jews. The Party leaders claimed that the Jews were linked with foreign imperialists and a menace to communist ideals.

Czechoslovakia struggled hardest and longest to maintain a democratic government. But in 1948 the Czechs were forced to submit to Soviet dictatorship. The country is rich in national resources and the people are industrious. The Soviet Union badly needed Czech production to build up its war-shattered economy. Stalin prevented the Czechs from holding free elections, imposed a totalitarian regime, and left few loopholes for outward expressions of nationalism.

However, at the time of the Polish demonstrations, the Czechs also launched a campaign for freedom of expression and greater democracy. In contrast to Poland, where the Party clamped down on political change, Czech Party leaders responded to popular demand and took charge of the reform movement. They brought about a revolution within the Party, but did not try to overthrow communism. Party government changed hands, and the new leaders stood for a far more liberal policy than their predecessors. They made it clear that though they wanted to remain on friendly terms with Moscow, they believed in personal liberty and coexistence with the West. Censorship was abolished, and men prominent in public life appeared on television to confront criticism. Many communist principles persisted and industry remained under public ownership, but the bloodless revolution made a big step forward in the direction of democratic socialism.

Party leaders in Moscow regarded the new regime in Prague as a threat to Soviet supremacy. In a press and radio campaign they accused Czech liberals of pandering to Western imperialists, and in the summer of 1968 they carried out menacing army maneuvers in and around Czechoslovakia. However, Alexander Dubcek, Secretary of the Czech Communist Party, and his liberal supporters were not intimidated. They stoutly defended their right to national liberty within the socialist sphere. Early in August they were summoned to a summit meeting with Soviet, Bulgarian, Hungarian, East German and Polish Party leaders at Bratislava, on the border of Hungary. After tense discussion all six powers signed a communique recognizing Czech sovereignty while proclaiming socialist solidarity. It seemed that the Czechs had won the right to choose their way of life, and that Soviet leaders were capable of adapting communist rule to current conditions.

But on August 20 Soviet forces invaded Czechoslovakia. The following morning people in Prague awoke to the roar of tanks and planes. Dubcek was arrested and the parliament building occupied. Young patriots protested and some were killed. Soviet and satellite troops streamed into the country. After days of agonizing uncertainty it was announced from Moscow that Dubcek and other Czech leaders were in conference there. Under Soviet pressure they were forced to agree to military occupation until conditions were "normal"; and to put the Communist Party and working-class power above all else. The tragedy of Budapest 1956 was repeated in Prague 1968. But, whatever happens in Czechoslovakia, Moscow lost much hitherto loyal support. The main communist parties in the West openly denounced Soviet action and world communism was weakened by dissent.

In September 1967 at the opening of the Twenty-Second Session, Corneliu Manescu, the Foreign Minister of Rumania, was elected President of the General Assembly of the United Nations. He was the first representative of a communist country to occupy the post. The Rumanian Government has handled its relations with the United Nations, and also with the Kremlin, with moderation and success. Rumanians have taken up a neutral stand in the ideological battle between Moscow and Peking, and have slowly but surely established economic and cultural ties with the West, even including West Germany.

The tiny mountain state of Albania is the poorest and most backward in Europe. At the end of the Second World War it was closely integrated with Yugoslavia and predominantly communist. In the Soviet-Yugoslav quarrel of 1948, Albania took the side of the Soviet Union, but the friendship soon broke up. The Albanians reacted against far-reaching Soviet demands and threw in their lot with communist China, the only people in Europe to do so. It seems unlikely that they want to embark on a crusade of permanent revolution hand-in-hand with Mao Tse-tung, but they probably prefer the remote control of Peking to the communist watchdogs from Moscow sapping their meager resources. Although President Tito attended the fiftieth anniversary conference in Moscow, the Albanians expressed their independence by staying away.

Fifty years after the Bolshevik Revolution, the Caribbean island of Cuba is the only communist-held state in the western hemisphere. It is ruled by Fidel Castro, a guerrilla fighter who became a supreme dictator. He won his position by force of arms, backed up by the antagonism of the impoverished peasant population to a corrupt and cruel dictatorship. In 1961, when Castro seized power, he blamed all Cuba's troubles on the United States and established ties with communist Russia. He made a secret agreement with Khrushchev permitting the construction of launching sites for long-range ballistic missiles on the island, and when they were later dismantled under American pressure he felt betrayed and humiliated by his communist partner. Castro turned to Red China to heal his wounded pride until he discovered Mao's plans to control the communist movements in Latin America as well as in Asia and Africa. Castro shares Mao's belief in the value of violence and perpetual struggle, but he is determined to direct guerrilla operations in the Latin American countries from his headquarters in Cuba, with no Russian or Chinese interference.

There were, in 1967, two rival revolutionary currents in Latin America: the official communist parties, whose members followed the Russian line and opposed the theory of inevitable war; and, secondly, groups of local guerrillas led by Castro's agents who aimed at creating widespread chaos as a prelude to communist take-over. These bands of jungle fighters proudly called themselves the Army of Liberation and they went into action in Colombia, Venezuela, Guatemala and Bolivia at Castro's command. In Bolivia in October 1967 a Cuban-inspired guerrilla operation was defeated by the Bolivian army and the leader, Che Guevara—a political adventurer who had worked closely with Castro for many years—was reported captured and killed. So far Castro's extremists have not succeeded by their armed attacks in converting a single government to Cuban communism.

The situation inside Red China is a matter of constant analysis, surmise and some guesswork on the part of the outside world. But there seems little doubt that widespread political confusion and economic depression followed the cultural revolution. Mao evidently tried to eliminate "revisionist" tendencies by

Reading news of the cultural revolution

forming a network of revolutionary committees throughout the Chinese provinces, composed of reliable Party members, loyal units of the army and of the newly recruited Red Guards. But the members of the committees could not agree and the more disciplined communists found the Red Guards unruly partners. Presumably Mao eventually saw the folly of handing out guns to untrained teenagers, for he reinforced the authority of the regular army and issued orders forbidding the distribution of any more arms.

Lin Piao, the Minister of Defense who was named successor to Mao Tse-tung, made a speech to the nation praising the achievements of the cultural revolution. He admitted some setbacks, but claimed that the gains were far greater than the losses. He did not however present a public balance sheet to support his optimistic statement. In the autumn of 1967 the People's Daily, the official Party paper, stated that "the immense spiritual force, generated by the great proletarian cultural revolution, has been transformed into a gigantic material force propelling forward the development of socialist construction." Ardent Maoists credited Chinese nuclear progress, culminating in the explosion of an H-bomb in June 1967, to the inspiration of the cultural revolution. Other, more critical, students of Chinese affairs suggest that this is wishful thinking. They say that the nuclear scientists, working away in secret behind closed doors, were probably the last people to be affected by the general upheaval.

When Chou En-lai returned to China after a visit to Africa in 1963 he reported that the newly independent, underdeveloped nations there "were ripe for revolution." But they did not respond as Mao hoped to the gospel of violence. Fired by intense nationalism, these subject peoples had fought for, and won, their freedom from colonial rule. But once they are independent the prospect of perpetual struggle no longer appeals to them. They want good jobs, homes for their families, education and enough to eat. Many young Africans have studied in capitalist countries and observed the way of life. Bicycles, cars, radios and watches have become symbols of success. Moreover the rulers of the new nations see clearly that it is entirely against their personal interests to stir up internal revolutions that could only result in their own downfall and replacement by ardent party leaders under Chinese influence.

In May 1968 student demonstrations broke out in France and many other European countries. In Paris the rioters seized the Sorbonne University and the national theater, set up barricades and fought the police. Many student leaders were inspired by the Maoist Red Guard movement, but their following included anarchists, Castroites and other extreme revolutionaries. Only in France did they succeed in persuading the workers to declare a strike which brought the life of the country almost to a standstill. But the orthodox Communist Parties refused to join in, partly because they did not want to submit to student leadership and partly because, according to communist standards, the countries were not ripe for revolution. In a few weeks the demonstrations petered out and the strikers went back to work in return for promises from President de Gaulle to bring in widespread reforms.

In the West the strength of the communist parties has steadily declined from the peak period after the war. The resistance groups, many of them under communist command, no longer had a place in national life and social welfare became an essential part of every successful political party program.

The term "socialist" has lost its Marxist meaning in the West because the Socialist, or Labor, parties now stand for reform by parliamentary action instead of by outright revolution. Throughout the non-communist world, governments have introduced varying degrees of state ownership, nationalized education, health services, public transport, old age pensions, child allowances and unemployment benefits. They have diminished the privilege of inherited wealth by graduated estate taxes, limited retained earnings and graduated income taxes. They are, in fact, slowly steering the structure of society toward the economic equality that Marx desired.

There is however a fundamental difference in outlook between people who believe in freedom of speech, open elections and government by the political party of their choice, and those who accept a totalitarian state and police rule—the current expression of Marxism.

In Russia Khrushchev's dictatorship was followed by the dual leadership of Aleksei Kosygin as Premier of the Soviet Union, and Leonid Brezhnev as Secretary of the Party. Both men had served under Stalin and Khrushchev, and probably survived the purges because they were technicians as well as politicians and had played a useful part in industry. They took office without bloodshed or any great political fanfare. They abandoned Khrushchev's most dramatic agricultural schemes; but, to begin with, they adopted his foreign policy and kept up contact with the West.

Kosygin, like Khrushchev, was a traveler. He appeared to believe in the policy of coexistence between nations. He flew to London to meet Mr. Harold Wilson, Prime Minister of Great Britain; to Paris to interview General Charles de Gaulle, President of France; to Cuba to contact Fidel Castro, Premier of Cuba; and to the United States to discuss East-West problems with President Lyndon Johnson.

Premier Kosygin and President Johnson meet in Glassboro, New Jersey, in 1967

In July 1967, in the quiet little college town of Glassboro, New Jersey, the Premier of the Soviet Union and the President of the United States spent a weekend talking over what Kosygin later described as "a little bit about everything." The peace-loving people of the world watched and waited hopefully for East-West settlement of the two outstanding crises of the day: the Vietnam war and the long-standing deadlock between Israel and the Arab nations in the Middle East. They prayed too for a treaty to stop the spread of nuclear arms. Later, when it was apparent that no major peace decisions had been made, they tried to find comfort from the fact that the meeting had taken place at all.

The Iron Curtain has slowly been drawn aside and foreigners are encouraged to visit the Soviet Union. They are not free to wander at will, but they do have a chance to see the outward form of modern Marxism in action. Party discipline is more lenient, police methods milder, and material rewards for good communists larger even than in Khrushchev's day. Books and newspapers are still censored, and liberal views likely to be severely punished, but on the other hand, the Soviet Union sends delegates to international cultural and scientific conferences and teams to compete in sporting events. As a result of increased prosperity Russian housewives find the shops are better stocked each year. Food is more plentiful, equipment more varied, and fashions more exciting every season. Goods are very expensive, but as there is no surplus almost everything sells.

The emphasis on youth is still predominant. There is no relaxation in educational programs either in or out of the classroom. School boys with red ties and school girls with red head scarves, carefully drilled for group action, take part in Party rallies. In the jubilee parade a regiment of marching soldiers carried small children high on their shoulders; each child brandished

Pilgrimage to the Lenin Mausoleum

a red star. From childhood onward Russians are exposed to a barrage of neon lights and Party posters inciting them to greater and greater effort, and urging them to take greater and greater pride in Soviet success.

Few Russian churches are open today and the congregations are mainly elderly and infirm. For the younger communists the cult of Lenin has taken the place of orthodox religion. The image is built up with statues and portraits of Marx and Lenin, most bearing inscriptions and many decked with wreaths. Day after day the waiting line to enter the Lenin Mausoleum is twelve pilgrims wide and up to a mile long, besides the foreign tourists who get special passes.

A British and an American student toured Russia by car in the summer of 1967. They followed a restricted route arranged by Intourist, the Soviet organization which deals with foreign visitors. They were well aware that they were under constant police supervision, but nevertheless, by devious means, they managed to talk to Russians of their own age. They communicated in a mixture of Russian, French and English and found a staggering ignorance of Western ways, but also an intense curiosity and a fantastically high value on Western products. They traded the only Western popular record they possessed for twenty-five Russian classical records and the Russians set the exchange rate. Before they left the country the Western boys were wise enough to realize that the interest in their way of life was secondary to unshakeable faith in Russian greatness and rightness, and pride in the superiority of communism over all other forms of government. Most young Russians have absorbed their socialist teaching with unquestioning faith. They are convinced that the Soviet Union is the most powerful state in the world because it is a living expression of patriotic endeavor; and they are satisfied that communism is the best way of life that any nation can offer. They are openly anti-Chinese and appalled by the fear that Mao Tse-tung could involve them in a third world war.

Karl Marx built up his blueprint for world revolution from a life study of historical development and change, which he attributed to a sequence of contradictory processes. In the following century his own theories were contradicted by the spread of modern scientific discovery. When Marx demanded the total destruction of the then existing system of society as the only possible prelude to the creation of a harmonious classless world, he had no concept of the effect of one atomic bomb. Feudalism was overtaken by capitalism and Marxism was overtaken by the nuclear age, and by liberal reformist movements.

There will probably never be a clear-cut judgment on Marxism. To many millions of people it is a religion, to many other millions it is an ugly threat. It is weakened from within by the conflicting doctrines of Russian and Chinese communist schools of thought. Some Russians have ceased to believe that war is inevitable and they preach coexistence as the only hope of survival. The Chinese, on the contrary, still believe in the absolute inevitability of war between communist and capitalist nations and cling to the principle of world revolution. The fate of civilization hangs in the balance, but whatever the eventual outcome, most philosophers and historians today accept the teaching of Karl Marx as a timely challenge to capitalist complacency and exploitation, and an impetus to social reform. And they agree that by his force of intellect and inflexible purpose, Marx has contributed to the advancement and knowledge of mankind.

Bibliography

Alliluyeva, Svetlana. *Twenty Letters to a Friend.* New York: Harper & Row, Publishers, 1967.

Cornforth, Maurice. *Introduction to Dialectical Materialism.* Vol. I: *Materialism and the Dialectical Method,* 1960. Vol. II: *Historical Materialism,* 1962. Vol. III: *Theory of Knowledge,* 1963. New York: International Publishers Co., Inc.

Crankshaw, Edward. *Khrushchev: A Career.* New York: Viking Press, Inc., 1966.

Deutscher, Isaac. *Stalin: A Political Biography.* New York: Oxford University Press Inc., 1949.

The Essential Left: Four Classic Texts on the Principles of Socialism. Marx, Engels and Lenin. London: Unwin Books, 1962.

Fall, Bernard B. *The Two Vietnams: A Political and Military Analysis.* New York: Frederick A. Praeger, Inc., 1967.

Fisher, H. A. L. *A History of Europe.* Vol. II: *From the Beginning of the Eighteenth Century to 1937.* Mystic: Lawrence Verry Inc., 1963.

Frankland, Mark. *Khrushchev.* New York: Stein & Day, 1967.

Hudson, F. G., Lowenthal, Richard and MacFarquhar, Roderick. "The Sino-Soviet Dispute," *The China Quarterly.* London, 1961.

Hunt, R. N. Carew. *The Theory and Practice of Communism.* Baltimore: Penguin Books, Inc., 1963.

Lichtheim, George. *Marxism: An Historical and Critical Study.* New York: Frederick A. Praeger, Inc., 1961.

MacIver, R. M. *The Modern State*. New York: Oxford University Press, 1926.

Mehnert, Klaus. *Peking and Moscow*. New York: Mentor-New American Library, 1963.

Nettl, J. P. *The Soviet Achievement*. New York: Harcourt, Brace and World, Inc., 1968.

O'Ballance, Edgar. *The Red Army of China*. New York: Frederick A. Praeger, Inc., 1964.

Royal Institute of International Affairs. *The Impact of the Russian Revolution 1917–1967*. Introductory essay by Arnold J. Toynbee. New York: Oxford University Press, 1967.

Schlesinger, Ina and Blustain, Jonah. *Communism: What It Is and How It Works*. New York: The Macmillan Company, 1964.

Schram, Stuart. *Mao Tse-tung*. New York: Simon & Schuster, Inc., 1967.

Shah, Sirdar Ikbal Ali. *Viet Nam*. London: The Octagon Press, 1960.

Shub, David. *Lenin: A Biography*. Baltimore: Penguin Books, Inc., 1966.

Ulam, Adam B. *Lenin and the Bolsheviks*. London: Secker & Warburg, 1966.

Wint, Guy. *Communist China's Crusade*. New York: Frederick A. Praeger, Inc., 1965.

Index